SHALOM!

THE BIBLICAL CONCEPT OF PEACE

DOUGLAS J. HARRIS

BAKER BOOK HOUSE ● Grand Rapids, Michigan

Preface

In his second inaugural address, January 21, 1957, President Eisenhower said, "We seek peace in a climate of freedom. It may be the only climate possible for life itself!" He went on to say that there must appear the spark of hope for progress or there would surely arise at last the flames of conflict. President Eisenhower followed this up in his State of the Union message, January 9, 1958, by calling for "Works of Peace." He said that we should come to know and understand one another. We should cooperate in works of human welfare. We should move toward using science for peace.

The *Christian Century,* May 29, 1957, printed a suggestion of two distinguished English Quakers, Barrow Cadbury and Professor Kathleen Lonsdale, that each nation appoint a "minister of peace and good will" distinct from the office of secretary of state or foreign minister. This may be one of those simple suggestions that after a while bears fruit. No nation, to my knowledge, has yet appointed such a minister. We have seen the development of a Peace Corps with a world outreach.

The *Kansas City Star,* January 2, 1967, carried an article about Ali Barzegar, a Moslem doing graduate study at the University of Oklahoma. He felt that science based on empiricism alone has produced great technology with no values or sense of morality. "It has advanced," he said, "to the extent that science can wipe mankind out and can wipe out all peace in human life. I think peace in human life is gone."

In the same article, Mr. Bowadikji, a mechanical engineer, asked, "The societies we are trying so hard to copy, what do they really have to offer? Man is turned into a production tool."

The *Asian Student,* March 9, 1968, told how on February 28 young people from thirty countries mingled handfulls of earth from all over the world and laid the foundation of "Auroville," a universal cultural township being created near Pondicherry, South India. This "first world city" on the Madras-Pondicherry border will house 50,000 people of every nationality. The project is sponsored by the Aurobindo Society of Pondicherry, in memory of Sri Aurobindo, the Indian philosopher. Auroville is to be set up at a 15-square-mile site surrounded by three lakes and the sea. Plans for the international city have been drawn by a consortium of French architects. It is to be "a universal town where men and women of all countries will be able to live in peace and progressive harmony, above all creeds, all politics, and all nationalities . . . a place of peace, concord and harmony, where man's aggressive instincts will be diverted into constructive channels, and used to vanquish suffering and misery, overcome human weakness and ignorance, triumph over human limitations and shortcomings." That an attempt can be made to actualize such a dream is in itself encouraging.

Voices from drama, fiction, poetry and the pulpit remind us that we have entered a new and critical era. The choices that are before us are staggering. Is the human race to survive or decline? Are we at the beginning or the end? We face great danger and unparalleled opportunity. Most agree that our crisis is not primarily material, economic or intellectual. It is a moral and spiritual crisis.

This is the time for a great reconciliation to take place, between men and God, and among men and within men. There is guidance for this in a study of *The Biblical Concept of Peace.*

Despair, pessimism and the terrific weight of materialism

and godlessness press upon us. It is not easy to cultivate hope. Yet, if there are individuals of true faith and commitment, each living and working in his own small corner of the world, who knows what new light may shine forth? God may yet lead us in paths of peace. In many Jewish synagogues today the Sabbath service concludes with, "The Lord God bless his children and all mankind with peace."

Peace movements and peace offensives have often been perverted and subverted, yet the plain man wants peace. He wants the amplitude of peace envisioned in the Bible. The real basis for peace is spiritual. Hope for peace lies in spiritual progress. It is my objective that this study may open the way just a little toward spiritual understanding and assimilation of this basic biblical concept. . . .

PEACE

Contents

Introduction

From June 1955 to May 1956 our family lived in Edinburgh, Scotland. Our three children went to school, and my wife and I attended the lectures at New College, the University of Edinburgh.

It was our privilege to hear and come to know personally Professors John Baillie, William Manson, Norman W. Porteous, and James S. Stewart. It was at this time that I first became interested in the subject *The Biblical Concept of Peace*. It was officially accepted as a thesis subject by the University, and I proceeded to gather material. Dr. Lamb, the Librarian at New College, was most helpful, as was Miss Erna R. Leslie.

I returned to my teaching responsibilities at Carson-Newman College, Jefferson City, Tennessee, and continued to work on the subject in my spare time. The library at Carson-Newman was quite useful, and the Librarian, Miss Mildred Iddins, secured books for me through Inter-library Loan. My good friend, Dr. Leo T. Crismon, Librarian at Southern Baptist Theological Seminary, Louisville, Kentucky, made books available that were needed.

During the summers of 1961 and 1962 several weeks were spent at the libraries of Emory University, Atlanta, Georgia, and Vanderbilt University, Nashville, Tennessee. Personnel at both places went out of their way to be of assistance. Conversation and correspondence with Professor Gerhard von Rad while he was in the United States in 1960-61 was particularly helpful, since he wrote the Old Testament treatment of "Peace" in Kittel's *Wörterbuch* which I had worked through while at Edinburgh.

The breadth of this subject has been its greatest problem, especially in taking hold and giving it form and order. After a while some limitations had to be made. The Bible itself has much material on this subject. The Jewish Apocrypha and extra-canonical apocalyptic literature had to be left out, as did the Dead Sea Scrolls. Undoubtedly there is development here which would be interesting to trace. For example, in the *Manual of Discipline* the righteous are promised eternal peace.

Every passage in the Bible having a bearing on this subject was studied in context, first in Hebrew and Greek and then in English. The best available commentaries were used. To this study was related other reading of which the Bibliography is a record. Again, sifting, selection and limitation were necessary, if there was to be any hope of unity and coherence. Exploration of technical and analytical problems was held to a minimum and sometimes simply indicated in footnotes. A glance at the Table of Contents will outline for the reader the scope and development of the subject.

The Bibliography includes not only books quoted or referred to in the footnotes, but also other books which relate to the subject and which might be helpful in future exploration. At the time the Bibliography was prepared I did not have all the information on books I had read and noted from various places. In particular, there are some books concerning which I failed to note the total number of pages.

I dedicate the book to my wife, as unique as her name, Zenona . . . helper, critic, source of encouragement and inspiration.

Douglas J. Harris
William Jewell College

SHALOM!

I. An Iridescent Concept

A drive is under way to build a monument to be named "Statue Shalom" on Mount Carmel overlooking the Haifa harbor in Israel.[1] The project has evoked comparison with New York harbor's Statue of Liberty. On a plaza in front of Tokyo Station stands a robust statue with arms stretched heavenward. On its base is inscribed, in Greek and Japanese, the single word, *Agape*.[2] These are doubtless matched in various parts of the world by other expressions of the deep longing on the part of human beings for the simple verities that make life meaningful.

Many people say "Good-bye" without thinking of the theological connotation, "God be with ye." Paul has "Grace to you and peace" as a part of the salutation in every one of his letters, yet people read this singular combination repeatedly without much thought. In ten of the letters associated with Paul's name we have an added phrase which tells us that this grace and peace is "from God our Father and the Lord Jesus Christ."

People of Semitic background in the Near-East greet those they regard as true brethren with *shalom*. Where there is any barrier, the greeting is impossible. An Arab student at the University of Tennessee said that *shalom* meant, "may that which is good within you richly abound and flow out to those around you." This is a meaningful greeting, and yet the word means much more. Gerhard von Rad[3] used the German word *schillerndes* to describe *shalom*. The best

13

English equivalent of *schillerndes* is "iridescent." This concept is many-colored like the rainbow.

Digging into the biblical concept of peace starts with this basic Hebrew word *shalom*. Not counting various proper names[4] such as Salem, Jerusalem, Absalom and Solomon, there are more than 350 appearances of *shalom* or its derivatives in the Old Testament.[5]

The root meaning is "to be whole, sound, safe." The fundamental idea is totality. God is the source and ground for *shalom*. Anything that contributes to this wholeness makes for *shalom*. Anything that stands in the way disrupts *shalom*.

Shalom and Community

Shalom makes for community. Loneliness, the lack of community, the Old Testament only knows as something unnatural, an indication that life is failing. The ones who suffer speak of being alone. Jeremiah says, "I sat alone, because thy hand was upon me" (15:17).[6] The Psalmist cries out, "I am like a vulture of the wilderness, like an owl of the waste places; I lie awake, I am like a lonely bird on the housetop" (102:6-7). In describing the willfulness and misery of his people, Hosea says that Israel is like "a wild ass wandering alone" (8:9). This animal usually goes in a drove, the bird belongs in its flock, and when they are alone, they are abandoned. So it is with human beings.[7]

Community involves common participation in the blessings of God. In the community which enjoys *shalom*, there is harmony and opportunity for the free untrammelled growth of the individual. This growth finds encouragement through the helpful inter-relationship of persons. "There is 'totality' in a community when there is harmony, and the blessing flows freely among its members, everyone giving and taking whatever he is able to."[8]

The wholeness and well-being of the community is endangered by a selfish and deceptive act like that of Achan (Josh. 7). There was tension in the friendship of David and Jonathan because of the hostility of Saul toward David.[9] There was a lack of *shalom* in David's own family, particularly centering in Absalom, whose name, ironically, means "father of *shalom*."[10] There is particular poignancy in David's inquiry, "Is it *shalom* with the young man Absalom?" (II Sam. 18:29-32).

When Solomon in his prayer of dedication appeals to the people, "Let your heart therefore be *wholly true* to the Lord our God" (I Kings 8:61), the word translated "wholly true" is *shalem*. Later on, Solomon's heart was not "wholly true" (I Kings 11:4).

In Psalm 41:12 the Psalmist believed God had upheld him because of his *integrity*. Here again the root is *shalom*. In Psalm 119:165 we read, "Great *shalom* have those who love thy law; nothing can make them stumble." With *shalom* like this, wholeness and integrity are developed in the individual, and this makes for *shalom* in the community.

The idea of "paying double" and "making restitution," particularly brought out in the American Standard Version of the requirements in Exodus 22, indicates an ethical obligation necessary for restoring *shalom*.

Absence of Shalom

In his oracle concerning Egypt, Isaiah (19:2) says, "and they will fight, every man against his brother and every man against his neighbor." Micah (7:5-6) sees this loneliness and distrust bringing ruin in his day — "a man's enemies are the men of his own house." Jeremiah experienced the same aloneness — "All my familiar friends (my men of *shalom*) watching for my fall" (20:10). There is a reaching toward New Testament thinking in Jeremiah's letter to the exiles — [9] "But seek the *shalom* of the city where I have sent you into exile, and pray to the Lord on its behalf, for in its *shalom*

you will find your *shalom*" (29:7). In the same letter God
then promises (29:11) that He has "plans for *shalom* and
not for evil, to give you a future and a hope." The Psalmist
is moved through his feeling of loneliness to a fuller trust in
God (31:13-16). In another place he is distressed because
his "bosom friend" (man of *shalom*) ". . . has lifted up his
heel against me" (41:9). This is the opposite of *shalom*.
When the "man of *shalom*," the one who shares one's bread,
the one on whom another relies, turns to treachery, then
shalom is gone. When enmity comes from one who is close
and trusted there is nothing on which to build wholeness
and community.

Shalom as Inner Peace

Professor von Rad states that there is not any Old Testament reference in which *shalom* denotes the specific psychical
condition of an inner peace.[11] This thought-provoking statement makes one try to think of possible exceptions. In
Jeremiah 30:5 we read, "Thus says the Lord: We have
heard a cry of panic, of terror, and of no peace. . . ." That
this lack of peace may include a loss of inner peace may be
indicated by the question at the end of verse 6, "Why has
every face turned pale?" Isaiah (32:17) prophesied of the
day when "the effect of righteousness will be peace, and the
result of righteousness, quietness and trust for ever." The
"great peace" promised those who "love thy law" (Ps. 119:
165) could be along the line of inner peace. Also the Septuagint rendering of Haggai 2:9 adds the phrase, "even
peace of soul for a possession to every one that builds, to
raise up this temple."[12] Though these words were probably
not in the original Hebrew text, they reflect thinking about
"peace of soul" in the post-exilic period.

Professor von Rad cites Lamentations 3:17, "my soul is
bereft of peace," as illustrating that *shalom* is more often related to a group than to an individual.[13] This is, of course,

an expression of Zion's sorrows. He is no doubt correct in saying that *shalom* is in its most frequent usage a social concept.[14]

Shalom and Health

It is easy to see how the root meaning of wholeness would relate to health and well-being. Jacob inquires concerning Laban, "Is it well (*shalom*) with him?" And they answer, "It is well" (Gen. 29:6). The common greeting or salutation of *shalom* (I Sam. 10:4; I Chron. 18:10) is wishing for the health, the well-being, the *shalom* of the one greeted. When a man is ill, there is no health (*shalom*) in his bones (Ps. 38:3). When he is in conflict with those who ought to be closest to him, there is no sense of wholeness: his feeling of community and even his integrity are threatened. Without using the word "psychosomatic," the Hebrews realized that spiritual, mental and emotional strains were related to one's health and well-being.

Shalom and Prosperity

The story of Joseph illuminates *shalom* as prosperity at several points with some side glances at *shalom* in human relationships. When his brothers saw that Jacob loved Joseph more than all the rest, they could not speak peaceably (with *shalom*) to him (Gen. 37:4). A little later, Jacob, apparently unaware of this rising hostility, sends Joseph to see whether it is well (*shalom*) with the brothers and whether it is well (*shalom*) with the flock, that is, are they prospering? (37:14). In all of Joseph's troubles in Egypt God was with him. God brought prosperity to Potiphar's house because of Joseph (39:5). The Lord was with Joseph in prison (39:21). When Pharoah is troubled by a dream, it is God who through Joseph will give Pharoah an answer of peace (*shalom*) (41:16). When his brothers come seeking food, Joseph tells them that if they are "true men" (ASV 42:19) let one stay behind as a hostage. "True" here is *kenīm,* but it is rendered in the Septuagint with *eirēnikōs.* When the brothers return in fear because they have found in their sacks the money they had paid, Joseph says, "Peace (*shalom*) be to you, fear not: your God, and the God of your father, hath given you treasure in your sacks: I had your money" (ASV 43:23).

⊘   *Shalom,* translated "prosperity," is in poetic parallel with "wealth" in Isaiah 66:12. *Shalom* is the situation where, due to God's goodness, everything can follow its own proper, undisturbed course to success, or even despite disturbances,⁴ God moves to bring about *shalom.* Köhler[15] compares *shalom* to the Greek *harmonīa tōn pāntōn.* However, he says, there is a significant difference. There is a dynamic element in the Hebrew concept — the Hebrew mind sees everything prospering and growing. There is a static element in the Greek phrase — the Greek mind sees things in a carefully arranged and harmoniously integrated *kōsmos.*

Shalom and War

It is natural that we should think of peace as opposed to war, and this is not absent from the biblical concept. If an individual has *shalom,* he has health, wholeness, soundness and integrity. As he lives in harmonious relationship with his family, this contributes to *shalom.* The wider the covenant of peace extends, the more all-inclusive is *shalom.* Isaac's conflict with the servants of Abimelech comes to a peaceful conclusion because they realize that God is with Isaac (Gen. 26). When Jacob is running away from Esau, he makes a vow which includes the hope that God will one day bring him back to his father's house in *shalom* (Gen. 28:21). Hamor and the men of Shechem mistakenly think the sons of Jacob are peaceable (34:21). Later Jacob is angry with his sons and says, "Ye have troubled me to make me to stink among the inhabitants of the land" (KJV 34:30) because they have used the overtures of *shalom* deceptively.

The Israelites sought peace with Sihon, but he came out against them (Deut. 2:26 ff.). Sometimes to choose peace was to choose to become vassals of Israel rather than to be annihilated (Deut. 20:10 ff.). The Gibeonites sought peace through deception and wound up as "hewers of wood and drawers of water" (Josh. 9:23). However, this covenant of *shalom* which the Gibeonites made with Joshua caused five kings to unite against them and obligated Joshua to go to their rescue (Josh. 10). When most of the enemy was decimated, the people returned in *shalom* and "not a man moved his tongue against any of the people of Israel" (10: 21). The next chapter closes with "And the land had rest from war" (see also Josh. 14:15). Sisera fled to the tent of Jael, the wife of Heber, for there was *shalom* between Jabin and Heber, but Jael did not keep the *shalom* (Judg. 4: 17 ff).

David sought, perhaps unwisely, to have a relation of *shalom* with Abner (II Sam. 3:21-23). Joab would have none of this, for the personal reason of not wanting a rival, plus the fact that Abner had killed Joab's brother, but most of all because Joab was distrustful of Abner's switch in allegiance and was concerned for the *shalom* of the kingdom.

A thought-provoking use of *shalom* is in II Samuel 11:7. David has sent for Uriah and inquires of Uriah about the *shalom* of Joab, and the *shalom* of the people and the *shalom* of the war! The word *shalom* is repeated three times. The RSV renders this, "David asked how Joab was doing, and how the people fared, and how the war prospered."

Adonijah came to Bathsheba, the mother of Solomon (whose name means "peaceable"). Bathsheba said, "Do you come with *shalom?*" Adonijah answered, *"Shalom"* (I Kings 2:13 ff.). Whatever Adonijah's motives were in asking for Abishag, Solomon put the worst possible interpretation on this request; to him it was another bid for the kingdom. Adonijah must be eliminated. There could be no *shalom* with him alive.

As Solomon's wealth and power and wisdom increased he had *shalom* on all sides. Typical of this was the *shalom* he had with Hiram of Tyre, which clearly meant a relation of peaceful cooperation (I Kings 5:12). And so we read, "And Judah and Israel dwelt in safety, from Dan even to Beersheba, every man under his vine and under his fig tree, all the days of Solomon" (I Kings 4:25). This ideal picture of *shalom* was one on which the Hebrews looked back with nostalgia. It also provided the framework for a future hope.

We have a striking illustration of the dissolution of *shalom* in Israel when Jehu comes driving hard in his chariot to overthrow the house of Ahab (II Kings 9). Elisha is pictured as instigating this coup by sending one of his disciples to anoint Jehu, who had no linear claim to the throne. From Jehu's point of view, it seems he and his friends were already plotting along this line. They regard the prophet apprehensively and say, "Is all *shalom*? Why did this mad fellow come to you?" (II Kings 9:11). When they are told that Jehu was anointed king, they readily join in and proclaim, "Jehu is king." As Jehu drives his chariot furiously toward Jezreel, King Joram of Israel sends two messengers one after another who anxiously inquire, "Is it *shalom*?" Jehu's brusque reply is, "What have you to do with *shalom*? Turn round and ride behind me." Then Joram himself, accompanied by Ahaziah, King of Judah, went to meet Jehu. Joram asks, "Is it *shalom*, Jehu?" Jehu answers, "What *shalom* can there be, so long as the harlotries and the sorceries of your mother Jezebel are so many?" Then Joram reined about and fled, saying to Ahaziah, "Treachery, O Ahaziah!" Both Joram and Ahaziah are killed as they flee, and Jehu arrives in Jezreel. "Jezebel heard of it; and she painted her eyes, and adorned her head, and looked out of the window." As Jehu entered the gate, she said "Is it *shalom*, you Zimri, murderer of your master?" Though Jezebel met this situation with a certain defiant courage, she knew it was not *shalom*.

The Covenant of Shalom

The concept of *berith,* "covenant," would itself make a study. In order to relate *berith* to *shalom* a few facts should be summarized. The root of *berith* is "to cut." It was the custom in solemn covenants to pass between the divided parts of the victims (Gen. 15:10-18; Jer. 34:18). The idea of "eating together" is also basic to *berith*.[16] There is an Assyrian equivalent *beritu* which has the idea of "bond."[17]

A covenant could be between individuals as in I Samuel 18:3 and 23:18. Marriage is described as a covenant (Mal. 2:14). Kings could make a covenant (II Sam. 8:9-10 and I Kings 20:34), and a king could make a covenant with his people (II Kings 11:4). Tribes and nations could make covenants (Josh. 9:6). New combinations in a covenant relationship often created confusion in older covenants and brought about conflict.

Connected with a covenant were rights and obligations. Both parties were not always on the same footing. A covenant could be sealed by a handshake, a kiss or the eating of a meal. There was often the exchange of gifts. To accept a gift obligated a person. The word *shalmonim,* "gifts," is related to *shalom*. It sometimes meant "bribe," for gifts were sometimes given for an unworthy purpose. However, a gift could also seal a solemn covenant.

There are a number of references to a covenant that God makes with His people. Accompanying this covenant are promises and an obligation. The prophets cry out against the unfaithfulness of God's people, and some of them picture a new covenant which will be written on the heart (Hos. 2:19-20; Jer. 31:31-34; Ezek. 16:60-63; Isa. 61:8).

To describe a covenant as "a covenant of *shalom*" adds strength and deepens the meaning. *Berith* and *shalom* were linked so often that this phrase came to be something like an official term. Moreover, *shalom* has something to say about the character and quality of the covenant.

A covenant involves a certain community of will. Those who are united have a common aim. The one becomes "whole with" (*shalēm*) the other. We have already noticed how Solomon exhorted the people — "Let your heart therefore be wholly true (*shalēm*) to the Lord our God" (I Kings 8:61).

> Within the community of the family, it is the man to whom the others subordinate themselves, and within other communities where peace reigns, it is the chief to whom they submit. And when two parties unite in the covenant, the one will generally be a greater giver than the other. The covenant is always a psychic community, but within it everybody must give and take as much as he can.[18]

The covenant consists in doing good for one another and refraining from doing harm (Gen. 26:26-33). There is the obligation for mutual defense (Josh. 10). There is also the requirement of mutual confidence and common endeavor. The story of Dinah in Genesis 34 illustrates both the significance and the treacherous violation of a covenant of *shalom*. A covenant of *shalom* ideally should lead to *shalom* in its fullest meaning.

Shalom and Salvation

Much of what has been said correlates with the Hebrew understanding of salvation. Salvation is certainly God's gift. It is God in action on behalf of His people. Perhaps the outstanding example of God at work for the salvation of His people was the exodus from Egypt's bondage.

Salvation meant victory in the struggles with evil men and with nations. Pedersen says:

> The difference between peace and salvation is that peace is rather the lasting state of harmony and happiness, salvation the

momentary acquisition thereof. . . . This difference also implies that salvation more particularly denotes victory over one's enemies; but in reality it comprises all acquisition of happiness. Eliphaz describes the benefits conferred by Yahweh on the good in the following manner: "He giveth rain upon the earth and sendeth water upon the fields, to set up on high those that be low; that those which mourn may be exalted in salvation" (Job 5:10-11). On the other hand, he says about the wicked, "His children are far from salvation, and they are crushed in the gate, without anyone saving them" (Job 5:4). Like victory in the court of justice, rain and fertility are included in salvation.[19]

Hence, there is an interpenetration between the concept of salvation and the ideal of peace with its root word *shalom*.

A further word from Pedersen is illuminating here:

The opposite of salvation is trouble, *sārā*, the state of narrowness. The sick man obtains salvation when he is cured. "Save my soul!" cries the miserable man from his sick-bed when his bones are wasted away (Psalm 6:38). A sinner who acknowledges that he himself has caused Yahweh to break his bones, i.e., to strike him with illness, asks permission once more to rejoice at his Lord's salvation (Psalm 51:14). The girl who is subjected to violence (Deut. 22:27), the man who is persecuted by his enemies (Psalm 7:2; 40:14-15; 59:3), he who never succeeds in anything he undertakes, who is oppressed and plundered (Deut. 28:29-31), who suffers misery and hunger (Psalm 34:7) — all desire salvation, the attainment of the happy state when they are delivered from evil.[20]

Salvation, like *shalom*, meant wholeness and integrity. It meant the community joined together in a covenant with God which included the obligation of loving response to God's commands. The fruits of salvation were health, prosperity, well-being and long life. The result was joy and blessing that came from doing God's will.

Yet time and again God's people broke the covenant and became subject to God's judgment and the removal of *shalom* marked by defeat, disunity, distrust, alienation, poverty and misery.[21]

However, God never wholly abandons His people. Hosea portrays God's free forgiving love that calls His people to repentance and renewal. With *shalom,* as with salvation, there is a characteristic openness toward the future, a future which God will give.

Offerings and Shalom

Bringing offerings was a part of man's response to God's gift of forgiveness and salvation. The thank-offering was the highest kind of peace-offering. God condescended to be the guest of the offerer, receiving the breast as His portion of honor, and then relinquishing it to His servant the priest. Thus the repast was a pledge of blessed fellowship into which He would enter with His people. It was also a love-feast at which, besides the members of the family, the Levites participated (Deut. 12:18 and 16:11). In this last reference the needy were included. Peace-offering from the root, "to be entire," carries the idea of one who is in peaceful or friendly relation to another. It is a relation of integrity. The peace offering is older than the sin offering. Both the peace-offering and the burnt offering are in Judges, but not the sin offering. Later when the peace-offerings and also the burnt offerings appear in conjunction with sin offerings, the sin offerings are to be offered first (Lev. 9:18; Num. 6:16). Hence it seems the peace-offering is a declaration that a relation of perfect peace between God and the offerer is restored, by means of the atonement of the sin offering.

Summary

The many-sidedness of *shalom* has been illustrated to some extent. We turn next to the fact that God is the giver of *shalom.* Following this, a look at the eschatological implications of *shalom* will lead us to the New Testament fulfillment of some of the expectations.

NOTES

1. *Land Reborn,* Baehr, Karl, editor. New York: American Christian Palestine Committee, Sept.-Oct., 1958, p. 3 and May, 1961, p. 8.
2. *Fellowship,* Hassler, Alfred, editor. Nyack, N.Y.: Fellowship of Reconciliation, Nov. 1, 1960, p. 10. *Agape* is the highest expression for love in Greek.
3. Kittel, Gerhard, *Theologisches Wörterbuch Zum Neuen Testament.* Stuttgart: Verlag Von W. Kohlhammer, 1935, Vol. II, p. 400.
   Among the German synonyms for *shalom* are: *Friede, Gluck, Wohlergehen* and *Heil.* For example, Heil and Unheil are used in Isa. 45:7 where the RSV has "I make weal and create woe."
4. Porteous, Norman W., *Shalēm-Shalom,"* Glasgow University Oriental Society Transactions, Vol. X, 1940-41, pp. 1-7. Edited by C. J. Mullo Weir. Glasgow: Civic Press, Ltd., 1943. In this stimulating and suggestive paper Professor Porteous traces evidences in the Ras Shamra Tablets and elsewhere for the existence of a god *Shalēm* and his association with Jerusalem and such names as Absalom and Solomon. Punning on the name of Jerusalem was frequent. The association of the *shalom* motif with the messianic king is noted, for example in Isaiah and Zechariah. A carry-over is seen in such New Testament passages as: Luke 2:14; Eph. 2:14; Col. 3:15 and Phil. 4:7, and in the priest after the order of Melchizedek in Hebrews. Professor Porteous concludes that the association of the *shalom* motif with Jerusalem was in part responsible for the fact that when the Jews thought of the return of Paradisal conditions they depicted these in the form not of a garden but of a city of God.

   H. H. Rowley writing in *Festschrift Alfred Bertholet,* Tübingen: J. C. B. Mohr, 1950, an article entitled, "Melchizedek and Zadok," says, *"Shalēm* was a divine name, as is securely established by the Ras Shamra evidence." Rowley says Dussaud regards *Shalēm* as the god of the evening peace, represented by the evening star. He says Albright holds Shulman to have been the god of the Underworld. Rowley goes on to say that it is probable that *Sedek* was a divine name, though by the time of the Old Testament the word *sedek* had become ethicized. It was particularly associated with Jerusalem. Rowley quotes Cook as saying, "This persistent association of the idea of 'right' with Jerusalem carried with it ideas, beliefs and practices which were capable of profound development."
5. See Table in the Appendix giving all references. Key markings help to bring out the variety of meanings.
6. All quotations are from the *Revised Standard Version* of the

Bible, New York: Thomas Nelson and Sons, 1952, unless otherwise noted.

7. Pedersen, Johs., *Israel,* I-II, p. 263. London: Oxford University Press, first published 1926, reprinted 1954.
8. *Ibid.,* pp. 263-4.
9. *Ibid.,* pp. 279-85. Pedersen elaborates on this in detail.
10. *Ibid.,* pp. 265-70. Pedersen likewise elaborates on this.
11. Kittel, *op. cit.,* pp. 404-5.
12. *The Septuagint Version of the Old Testament and Apocrypha with an English Translation.* London: Samuel Bagster and Sons, Ltd.
13. Kittel, *op. cit.,* p. 405.
14. *Loc. cit.* See also Zech. 8:16 and Isa. 60:17.
15. Köhler, Ludwig, *Old Testament Theology,* translated by A. S. Todd. Philadelphia: The Westminster Press. (Lutterworth Press, 1957) Type set in G. B. Printed in U.S.A. This book originally appeared as *Theologie des Alten Testament,* Tübingen: J. C. B. Mohr, 1935. This translation has been made from the third revised edition, 1953, p. 240.
16. Gesenius, William, *Hebrew and Chaldee Lexicon of the Old Testament Scriptures.* With additions and corrections from the author's *Thesaurus* and other works, by Samuel Prideaux Tregelles. London: Samuel Bagster and Sons, 1867.
17. Richardson, Alan, *A Theological Word Book of the Bible.* London: SCM Press, Ltd., 1950.
18. Pedersen, *op. cit.,* p. 294.
19. *Ibid.,* p. 332.
20. *Loc. cit.*
21. Pedersen, *op. cit.,* pp. 288-92. Pedersen elaborates on this.

In this connection Jacob comments, "The justice of Yahweh is not the type of the blindfolded maiden holding a balance in her hand, the justice of Yahweh extends one arm to the wretch stretched out on the ground whilst the other pushes away the one who causes the misfortunes." Jacob, Edmond, *Theology of the Old Testament.* Translated by Authus W. Heathcote and Phillip J. Allcock. New York: Harper and Bros., 1958, p. 99.

II. God the Giver of Shalom

We have seen that *shalom* often includes the idea of material prosperity. However, when the word is used in its full meaning it is a religious concept. Material prosperity is often linked with spiritual well-being. God is the giver of *shalom*.

Gideon built an altar and called it "Yahweh-*Shalom*" (Judg. 6:24). God's gift of *shalom* is the climax in the prayer recorded in Numbers 6:24-26. This prayer is still frequently used as a benediction in worship services.

God makes *shalom* in His high heaven (Job 25:2). He is also one who guarantees *shalom* to man. He delights in the *shalom* of man, His servant (Ps. 35:27 and 147:14). *Shalom* is used three times in the call to prayer in Psalm 122: 6-9. The opening line in Hebrew has a beautiful poetic quality:

Sha-a-lu shalom Y-ru-shaw-lawm!

Though the etymology of Jerusalem is not a settled question, the most likely meaning is "men or people of *shalom*" or "habitation of *shalom*."[1] Here then is expressed the tension between the ideal and the real. The name stands for what this city is ideally meant to be. That *shalom* should become a reality is the prayer.

In Psalm 85:8 ff. God will "speak *shalom* to his people, to his saints, to those who turn to him in their hearts." Here *shalom* is linked with concepts of the highest spiritual meaning:

> Surely his salvation is at hand for those who fear him,
>   that glory may dwell in our land.
> Steadfast love and faithfulness will meet;
>   righteousness and *shalom* will kiss each other.

The word translated "steadfast love" in verses 7 and 10 is the Hebrew word *hesed,* on which Nelson Glueck has a significant monograph now available in English.[2] Here *hesed* appears in close relation with *shalom* and two other spiritual concepts "salvation" and "righteousness."

This hope that God will show His steadfast love in righteousness, that God will give salvation and *shalom* becomes a part of the eschatological hope of the Hebrews as will be seen later. The typological interpretation placed on Melchizedek in Psalm 110 and in the Epistle to the Hebrews is an example. (See particularly Hebrews 7:2.)

Hezekiah recognized that *shalom* comes from God. In his song of thanksgiving for being healed he says:

> Lo, it was for my *shalom*
>   that I had great bitterness;
> but thou hast held back my life
>   from the pit of destruction. . . .
> The living, the living, he thanks thee,
>   as I do this day (Isa. 38:17 and 19).

The Psalmist closes his evening prayer in the knowledge that Yahweh is the source of *shalom*:

> In *shalom* I will both lie down and sleep;
>   for thou alone, O Lord, makest me dwell in safety (Ps. 4:8).

Similarly in Psalm 29:11 (ASV):

> Jehovah will give strength unto his people;
> Jehovah will bless his people with *shalom*.

That *shalom* comes from God is seen again in Proverbs 16:7:

> When a man's ways please the Lord,
> he makes even his enemies to be at peace with him.

As is true of other gnomic sayings, this statement is not to be taken absolutely. God can do this, but sometimes it serves God's purpose that the righteous should suffer at the hands of his enemies and meet hostility with love, even when enmity is implacable.

According to the deuteronomic view, man could not expect to have *shalom* and continue to walk in the stubbornness of his heart. God would not permit this (Deut. 29:19-21). God gives, but God can also take away *shalom* (Jer. 16:5).

Paying vows to God, as in Psalm 116:14 and 18, has as its root the same verb from which we get *shalom*. This portrays man's response to God who gives *shalom*.

Jeremiah[3] and Ezekiel[4] are concerned about false prophets who keep proclaiming *shalom, shalom* when there is no *shalom*. There is no *shalom* because men are not right with God. Micah (3:5) speaks of prophets who cry *shalom* when they are well fed, but otherwise they declare war.

In Proverbs (3:13-17) the man who finds wisdom also walks in the paths of *shalom,* for both are a gift of God. So it can be readily seen that *shalom* was considered God's gift. This opens the way to think about the eschatological outreach of *shalom* which was God's promise for the future.

NOTES

1. In this connection see footnote 4 at the close of Chapter I.
2. Glueck, Nelson, *Hesed in the Bible,* translated by Alfred Gottschalk. Cincinnati, Ohio. The Hebrew Union College Press, 1967, especially pp. 79 ff. and 94 ff. The following summary of the significance of *hesed* is given in (212) DIGBY 9-4620, a brief description of Glueck's monograph by the KTAV Publishing House: *Hesed* is a word for a profound idea and ideal of mutual relationship of covenant character existing between man and man and man and God. In the human realm it is based on the reciprocal conduct and attitude that human beings, bound together by

blood or marriage or contractual relations or by the rules of
friendship and mutual decency and fair play and love evince towards each other. For the relationship between man and God it
involves obligations on the part of humans to God expressed
through moral and ethical conduct towards God's creatures, and
on the part of God through concern for and care of human beings
with whom he has entered a covenant relationship of law and
love. It is not subjective, one-sided loving kindness, charity or
grace, but rather the relationship of mutuality between the father-
hood of God and the brotherhood of man. It is not the love of
loyalty but the loyalty of love that *hesed* expresses and encom-
passes.

3. Jeremiah 6:14; 8:11, 15; 14:13; 23:17; 28:9.
4. Ezekiel 13:10, 16.

III. Eschatological Outreach

Eternal peace as a religious goal is only possible where a peace ideal of an ethical-religious or metaphysical kind has won significance for the whole conception of life. Though primitive religions show some interest in the dead, as evidenced by certain care in burial, the idea of eternal peace is not primarily primitive. Polytheistic nature religions show only rudimentary development in the eschatological concept of peace. Gradually there develops a deeper want for salvation beyond the wearing and restless struggles of this life. Under the pressure of sin and debts, persecution and sorrow, the vision of a transformed existence according to the will of God is understood as the goal of life. In religions of a strong ethical-social impulse the idea of a continuing relationship of community becomes a part of the vision. Israelite, Persian and Islamic religions hope for a state of perfection for the world in which the goal of God's rule for which they strive is reached. In different forms the peculiarity of each of these religions expresses itself in a significant manner. Islam was the least able to develop an inward connection between its religious possession and the peace of Paradise. Islam's consciousness of its commission aims so much at the establishment of a religious culture of compulsion in this world that the *dar ,el Salam* (house of Salvation or Paradise) is less aimed towards the perfection of the faithful community than to serve as a reward for faithful individuals. In Zoroastrianism there is a world-encircling contrast of good and evil which penetrates this world and the

31

other. Purpose and meaning in human life would be incomplete without the eschatological outlook towards a last decisive battle in which the kingdom of Ahura wins the victory. By this victory a new world of eternal life and eternal growth begins, free from old age, death, decay and rottenness. But this is at the same time a world of peace in which the moral missions of early life find their perfection.[1]

For the Hebrews the beginning of hope for the future may have been simply the desire of an early man of faith like Abraham to live a long and fruitful life and "go to his fathers in *shalom*" (Gen. 15:15). The symbol of Paradise was one means of envisioning the future. However, as we have already seen,[2] the concept of the City of God became a dynamic part of the future hope.[3] The symbolical element gives to the peace idea its supra-worldly character and guards against the error, which some persisted in anyway, that this ideal status can be reached empirically on this earth. This concept continued to develop in the late Jewish literature of the Apocrypha and Pseudepigrapha.[4] The New Testament development of this concept will be discussed later.

Throughout Israel's history the people were always falling short of their obligation in the covenant. It was hoped that they would find rest when Joshua led them into the promised land, but this turned out not to be true rest. The ups and downs in the period of the amphictyony[5] are an anticipation of further heights and depths. With David and Solomon there came hope of true *shalom,* but in the declining years of Solomon *shalom* began to slip, and in his son Rehoboam *shalom* was forfeited. The promise to the house of David (I Kings 2:33) was extended into the future. This is seen in Ezekiel 37:24-28, Micah 5:2-4 and many Psalms.

Connections of Israel's eschatological hope have been made with the Persian dualistic concept of two aeons.[6] However, there is considerable material in the Old Testament which portrays in a variegated manner this central theme that God has great blessings in store out in the future for His people. That the concept of *shalom* illuminates this hope can be illustrated with some selected examples.

The hope of future blessedness that God will provide is seen in Amos 9:11-15.[7] Though the word *shalom* is not used, much of the concept of *shalom* is here portrayed. In Acts 15:16-18 James quotes this passage as being fulfilled in his day with the Gospel reaching out to the Gentiles.

That this will be a time of great prosperity is envisioned in such passages as: Psalm 72:3; Isaiah 66:12-14; Jeremiah 33:9 and Zechariah 8:12. This is linked at first with the return from exile (Isa. 52:7-12; 54:11-17). Later the hope is projected further into the future so that the author of Daniel in the time of the Maccabean struggle gives a reinterpretation to Jeremiah's seventy years (Dan. 9).

A complete transformation of nature is envisioned in a number of passages: Hosea 2:18-23; Leviticus 26:3-13; Isaiah 11:1-10; 65:25; Ezekiel 34:25-31. Paul also catches a glimpse of this renewal of nature in Romans 8:22-25 and I Corinthians 2:9. We can trace the concept of "new heavens and a new earth" from Isaiah 65:17 and 66:22 on over to II Peter 3:13 and Revelation 21:1-5, which concludes with the emphatic declaration, "Behold, I make all things new!" Related to this is the picture of beating swords into plowshares and spears into pruning hooks in Isaiah 2:1-4 and Micah 4:1-4.

This outreach of spiritual anticipation has stimulated the hopes of men in many generations. Perhaps we can see some fulfillment in the peace which Jesus promised: "Peace I leave with you; my peace I give to you; not as the world gives do I give to you . . ." (John 14:27). Paul speaks of this as the "peace that passeth understanding" which can be as a fortress around the hearts of men even in troubled times (Phil. 4:7). However, men still dream of actually converting weapons of war into instruments of peace. On a building in the center of New York City is a bronze plaque depicting swords being melted into plowshares. However, in our day the weapons are not swords and spears! The potential for destruction and for good is multiplied almost beyond comprehension!

Righteousness and peace are linked frequently in the Old Testament: Isaiah 32:16-18; 48:17-19; 60:15-22; Psalm 72:7. More than once we are told "there is no *shalom* to the wicked" (Isa. 48:22; 57:21; 59:8). There is the messianic hope of the Prince of Peace (Isa. 9 and Zech 9:9), which is linked with the task of the servant (Isa. 52:13 — 53:12).

This eschatological outreach finds fulfillment and further projection in the New Testament.

NOTES

1. For thoughts expressed in this opening paragraph of Chapter III, I am indebted to an article on *Friede* by Eichrodt in: *Die Religion in Geschichte and Gegenwart,* Second Edition. Tübingen, 1928, J. C. B. Mohr; Gunkel and others, editors. Eichrodt compares the use of *pax* and *eīrēnē* by the Romans and Greeks. He refers to eternal *pax* as described by Seneca in *Consolatio ad Marciam* 19.4 He then speaks of the cosmic redemption religions which had in India and Greece their ripest development: Brahman, Buddhism, Hindu, Orphic and Neo Platonic. These cultivated a longing for peace of a metaphysical kind which was striving for a supra-cosmic solution of all dissonants into harmony by surrender of the outward relations of life: Nirvana, immortality, restoration of all. For the most part this was anti-social.

2. See Footnote 4, Chapter I.

3. For example: Haggai 2:6-9; Zephaniah 3:9 and other references noted later.

4. Charles, R. H., *Religious Development Between the Old and the New Testaments.* London: Oxford University Press, first published 1919 and continually reprinted.
   Rowley, H. H., *The Relevance of the Apocalyptic.* London: Lutterworth Press, first published 1944, second edition 1947.

5. This term denotes the religious confederacy during the time of Joshua and Judges. See Flanders, Crapps and Smith, *People of the Covenant.* New York: The Ronald Press Co., 1963, chapter 5 and especially p. 179.

6. Eichrodt, see Note 1 above.
   Leivestad, Ragnar, *Christ the Conqueror*: Ideas of Conflict and Victory. London: S.P.C.K., 1954.

7. This passage may reflect a formulation of this hope later than the time of Amos himself, perhaps in the exilic period.

IV. Pre-New Testament Connections

The Old Testament

The first three chapters were devoted to the development of the Old Testament concept. The root meaning of *shalom* is "to be whole, sound, safe," and the fundamental idea is totality. God is the giver of peace, the source and ground of *shalom*. *Shalom* makes for community, and Israel was at its best when the harmony, wholeness and well-being of the community was experienced by the people both qualitatively and quantitatively. The absence of *shalom* is an indication of hostility, enmity, distrust and trouble. *Shalom* has connotations of health and prosperity. The idea of peace as opposed to war is a part of the total concept of *shalom*. The connection of *shalom* with the Hebrew concepts of covenant, *hesed* and righteousness has been noted. Man brought peace-offerings to God. *Shalom* was often a synonym for what the Hebrew understood as salvation. In this connection it might be noted that from one of the root meanings, "submit oneself," especially to God, we get the participle "Muslim" and the infinitive "Islam," conveying the idea of submission to God.

One chapter was devoted to the eschatological outreach of *shalom*. This openness to the future, this hope that God has something in store for His people is a fundamental part of the Hebrew understanding of history and of God's purposes for the world.

The Septuagint

The Hebrew word *shalom* is rendered almost always in the Septuagint by *eīrēnē*. It was noted in Chapter I that *kenīm* is rendered in the Septuagint by *eirēnikos*. Ketchum[1] says that *eīrēnē* occurs 199 times in the Old Testament. He summaraizes: "Seven Hebrew words are translated in the Septuagint by *eīrēnē*. Five of these words are thus translated only one time each. Another, *batah,* meaning 'trust,' 'confidence,' 'security,' is expressed by *eīrēnē* nine times. In all the remaining examples, *shalom* with its cognate forms is the Hebrew word which is represented by *eīrēnē*.

However, what seems to be more important is the change in the content of *eīrēnē* which would come from using it so extensively in the Old Testament to translate *shalom*. This in itself would enrich the meaning of *eīrēnē* for early Christians who for the most part used the Septuagint more than the Hebrew Old Testament."[2]

Etymology

Eīrēnē is an old word. Its known history dates back to Homer.[3] Two different sources for the origin of *eīrēnē* are suggested by A. T. Robertson[4] and most lexicons. *Eīrēnē* may be either from *eīrō* "to join" or *eīrō* "to say." In either case the word implies a bond that is made, words that are spoken, as the basis on which peace rests.

Various scholars and lexicons are cautious as to which *eīrō* is the true source.[5] The idea of a bond or tie, and hence the concept of unity, is there. The English word "peace" may be traced through the Latin *pax,* the Greek stem *pag,* back to the Sanskrit *pac,* "to bind," "to fasten."[6]

Eīrēnē in the Classics

Ketchum[7] has a rather thorough treatment of the use of *eīrēnē* in the classics. He has quotations from Homer, Herodotus, Xenophon, Plato, Aeschines, Andocides, Demosthenes and Plutarch. He concludes that *eīrēnē* means "a state of harmony," "freedom from or cessation of war and strife." He points out that Peace was personified and worshiped as a goddess at Athens from 449 B.C. She was represented as being the daughter of Zeus and Themis (Hesiod, *Theogony,* 902). At a later period a temple to Peace was built in Rome by Vespasian (Josephus, *Wars of the Jews,* VII, 5, 7).

Eīrēnē in the Papyri and Inscriptions

A number of examples of *eīrēnē* in the papyri and inscriptions are available.[8] For the most part they illustrate the classical idea of "harmony," "concord," "freedom from strife," and the Hebrew idea of "well-being." Samples of Christian writings and inscriptions reflect the influence of the Septuagint and the New Testament on their thought and expression. One interesting example from the Oxyrhynchus Papyri (X. 129. 8) is of a father who breaks the engagement of his daughter and prospective son-in-law because of the latter's misconduct and his wish that his daughter lead a peaceful and quiet life. A common phrase in cemetery inscriptions of early Christains was *en eīrēnē.*[9]

NOTES

1. Ketchum, Henry Grady, *Eiphnh in the New Testament,* an unpublished thesis. Louisville, Ky.: The Southern Baptist Theological Seminary, 1933.
   See also, Hatch and Redpath, A Concordance to the Septuagint, Vol. I. Graz, Austria: Akademische Druck-V. Verlageanstalt, 1954.
2. Van Leeuwen, W. E., *Eiphnh in het Nieuwe Testament.* Wageningen: H. Veenman and Zonen, 1940. I had the loan of this monograph through the courtesy of Professor H. H. Rowley while in Edinburgh, 1955-56. With the assistance of a Dutch student I worked through it and translated portions of it. Reference will be made to it later. Van Leeuwen traces the background of *eīrēnē* in the Septuagint, Rabbinical Writings, Apocalyptic Writings and the Apocrypha. These last three areas are beyond the scope of my consideration as is made clear in my introduction.

3. Ketchum, *op. cit.,* p. 2. This monograph is primarily a word study, as the author himself states on p. v of the Preface. It is helpful in this chapter which I have entitled "Pre-New Testament Connections." My over-all indebtedness is hereby acknowledged. I have footnoted direct quotations. In connection with the origin of *eīrēnē* Ketchum says, p. 2, "The usual form in which it occurred was *eīrēnē,* though there were variations in the different dialects. The Doric form was *eirānā,* the Boetian was *irānā,* and the Pamphylian, *irēni.*

4. Robertson, A. T., *Paul's Joy in Christ.* New York: Fleming H. Revell Co., 1917, p. 54.

5. Ketchum, *op. cit.,* pp. 4-7. These pages contain a detailed etymological analysis.
   Arndt and Gingrich, *A Greek-English Lexicon of the New Testament and Other Early Christian Literature.* Chicago: University of Chicago Press, 1957, refers to an article on the history of *eīrēnē* by K. Brugmann and B. Keil.

6. Ketchum, op. cit., p. 5.

7. *Ibid.,* pp. 8-10.

8. *Ibid.,* pp. 21-23. A number of specific examples are given, such as names for officials. The Flinders Petrie Papyri (III.30.4) furnish an instance where *Eīrēnē* is a proper name. The name *Irene* comes from *Eīrēne.*

9. Two very interesting cemetery inscriptions are given by Ketchum on p. 23.

V. Peace and the Mission of Jesus

The prophecy of Zechariah[1] reflects prophetic passages from Malachi and Isaiah.[2] This portrait comes to a climax in the words, ". . . the day shall dawn upon us from on high to give light to those who sit in darkness and in the shadow of death, to guide our feet into the way of peace" (Luke 1: 78b-79).

The same hope is expressed in the angelic announcement, "Glory to God in the highest, and on earth peace among men with whom he is pleased."[3] Surely behind "peace" as used here is all the depth of spiritual meaning that we have already found in *shalom*. There is perhaps here at the outset an anticipation of Luke 19:38, "Blessed be the King who comes in the name of the Lord! Peace in heaven and glory in the highest!" That this good news is to *all people* is made clear in Luke 1:10.

Upon seeing the child Jesus, Simeon is ready to "depart in peace . . . for mine eyes have seen thy salvation" (Luke 2: 29-30). Here Simeon, like Anna, is representative of the simple, ordinary people of the land who rejoice that the hope of Israel is coming to fruition.

In the beatitude, "Blessed are the peacemakers: for they shall be called the children of God" (Matt. 5:9 KJV), Jesus sets forth a principle which is central to His mission and a challenge to those who would follow Him. The further implications of this principle are seen in Matthew 5:38-48. These verses on non-retaliation, on allowing one's self to be

imposed upon, on loving your enemies and praying for those
who persecute you have been used by extreme pacifists in an
absolute sense. These verses have sometimes been balanced
by the scene of Jesus cleansing the temple to illustrate a
time when even He resorted to force. Many have simply ig-
nored this part of the Sermon on the Mount. It is so human
to return evil for evil and to cherish enmity rather than rise
above it with forgiveness and love. We fail to see that Jesus
here is pointing to a better way.

In Mark 9:50b Jesus says, "Have salt in yourselves, and
be at peace with one another." To this one might relate His
instruction to the Twelve: "As you enter the house, salute
it. And if the house is worthy, let your peace come upon it;
but if it is not worthy, let your peace return to you" (Matt.
10:12-13; also compare Luke 10:5-6). Those who are open
to the message of the Gospel come to know the deep meaning
of peace. Those who do not respond miss out.

That peace relates not only to spiritual blessing but to
healing is seen in the healing of the woman who touched Jesus'
garment. Jesus says, "Daughter, your faith has made you
well; go in peace, and be healed of your disease" (Mark
5:34). Both the King James Version and the American
Standard Version have "be whole." Here is a fresh reminder
that wholeness is basic to the biblical concept of peace.
Compare Luke 7:50, where peace is associated with the
blessing of forgiveness.

In Luke 22:36 we have a later instruction of Jesus to the
Twelve that has puzzled Christians ever since: "But now, let
him who has a purse take it, and likewise a bag. And let
him who has no sword sell his mantle and buy one." Is Jesus
telling His disciples they must be prepared to defend themselves? In Matthew 26:52 He makes it clear that they are
not to defend Him: "Put your sword back into its place; for
all who take the sword will perish by the sword." In that day,
and almost to the present, it was the custom of men to carry
weapons of defense. Jesus may be trying to suggest to them

that the situation ahead will not be easy. When they say, "Look, Lord, here are two swords," and He replies, "It is enough" (Luke 22:38), it would seem He is certainly not overstressing this reliance on arms.

This leads to another statement of Jesus, "Do not think that I have come to bring peace on earth; I have not come to bring peace, but a sword" (Matt. 10:34).[4] One does not have to take the sword literally to recognize that Jesus speaks clearly here of the tension that is involved in following Him. This points to the central message of the cross, for on the cross there is one who is being pulled apart. Other evidences of cleavage that accompany discipleship are in such sayings as: "He who is not with me is against me, and he who does not gather with me scatters" (Luke 11:23), and "Not every one who says to me, 'Lord, Lord,' shall enter the kingdom of heaven, but he who does the will of my Father who is in heaven" (Matt. 7:21).

There are two remarkable statements of Jesus to His disciples as the time of the cross drew near which give us insight into His understanding of the word peace: "Peace I leave with you; my peace I give to you; not as the world gives do I give to you . . ." (John 14:27) and "I have said this to you, that in me you may have peace. In the world you have tribulation; but be of good cheer, I have overcome the world" (John 16:33). This first statement has been called the legacy of Jesus. What He gives is *not* as the world gives. This is not a placid peace. Peace here is not the absence of trouble. They are told to expect tribulation, but they may also contemplate victory!

All three synoptic Gospels recount the Royal Entry.[5] This incident provides an important key for our comprehension of Jesus' own understanding of His mission. To this we may well relate the passage He chose to read at Nazareth near the beginning of His ministry from Isaiah 61 (Luke 4:16-30). The prophetic picture in Zechariah 9 is of a King who comes in peace. This was *not* the popular messianic expec-

tation. Here, near the close of His ministry, Jesus offers Himself as God's anointed one, but in choosing the lowly ass and
being conscious of Zechariah's portrait of one who comes
in peace, He gave His interpretation of the kind of King He
came to be.[6]

There is much evidence in written word,[7] sign and symbol, that the cross is central to the mission of Jesus. Yet this
remains the hardest part of the Christian message to appropriate. Close to the center of the meaning of the cross is
the concept of Suffering Servant and connected with this is
the portrait of a King who comes in peace. These words of
Jesus are still hard to grasp: "But many that are first will
be last, and the last first" (Mark 10:31), and ". . . Whoever
would be great among you must be your servant, and whoever would be first among you must be slave of all. For the
Son of man also came not to be served but to serve, and to
give his life as a ransom for many" (Mark 10:43-45), and
"If any man would come after me, let him deny himself and
take up his cross and follow me. For whoever would save
his life will lose it; and whoever loses his life for my sake and
the gospel's will save it" (Mark 8:34b-35).

The cross speaks of tension, of a tearing apart. There is
suffering on behalf of and because of. There is a respond-
ing to hate and hostility with love. When Jesus said, "Father,
forgive them; for they know not what they do,"[8] He was not
suggesting that they be forgiven because they were ignorant.
They did not know the deep implications of what they did,
but there is plenty of evidence of enmity and hate. Jesus responded to this with the deep desire to forgive. This is the
only way to break the vicious circle of hostility. One particular prophetic picture stands out: "the chastisement of
our peace was upon him; and with his stripes we are healed"
(Isa. 53:5b KJV).

Peter refers to Jesus' message as the "good news of peace"
(Acts 10:36). Paul could say, "he is our peace" (Eph. 2:
14). The author of Hebrews could envision Jesus as a Priest

after the order of Melchizedek, King of Salem, that is, King of peace, Priest of God Most High (Heb. 7).

God's sign of victory of the cross is the resurrection.[9]

> The entire New Testament was written in the light of the resurrection fact. To all its writers, Jesus is the central figure of history, and they understand and interpret his career in the light of his resurrection. They regard this resurrection not merely as a possibility or even a probability; it is for them the one rock-bottom fact upon which the solid structure of the Christian faith and life is built.[10]

It was the risen Christ who could say three different times, "Peace be with you."[11]

NOTES

1. Luke 1:68-79. The father of John the Baptist. The name is spelled Zacharias in KJV.
2. Luke 1:78 and Mal. 4:5; Luke 1:78 and Mal. 4:2; Luke 1:79 and Isa. 9:2.
3. Luke 2:14. The alternate translation, "Peace, good will toward men." KJV does not have the support of the oldest MSS. However, particularly the rendering: "Peace, good will among men" has something to say about the quality of the peace that is challenging and probably reflects what peace had come to mean in the life of the early church.
4. Buttrick and others, editors, *The Interpreter's Bible.* New York: Abingdon Press, 1952, Vol. 8, p. 236. The authenticity of these passages in Luke and Matthew is here questioned. This may avoid the enigmatic drive of this saying, but the reasoning at this point is unconvincing.
5. Mark 11:1-10; Matt. 21:1-9; Luke 19:28-38.
   It has been noted that Matthew has two animals while Mark and Luke only one. Some suggest that Matthew mistakenly supposes that the Hebrew parallelism of Zech. 9:9, which he quotes, actually describes two animals. They go on to suppose that Matthew therefore has two animals, so that not even this detail of the prophetic picture will be different. However this may be, the further suggestion of some that this whole incident is manufactured by the early church as a fulfillment of prophecy is far more unconvincing than the straightforward understanding of Christ's mission. One is reminded of a statement of William Manson in his Preface, p. 8, to *Jesus the Messiah,* Philadelphia; Westminster Press, 1946:

"I have not in fact been able to accept the tacit assumption of the Form-Critics that the images and ideas by aid of which the post-resurrection Church represented to itself the person and work of its Lord were necessarily of the nature of makeshifts, the product of its own thought and life, and not his."

6. The connection between Luke 2:14 and Luke 19:38 was noted in the second paragraph of this chapter.

7. Of the countless books written to elucidate the message of the cross, I would like to mention:

Denney, James, *The Death of Christ*. London: Hodder and Stoughton, Second Edition, 1902.

Manson, William, *Jesus the Messiah*. Philadelphia: Westminster Press, 1946.

Wolf, William J., *No Cross, No Crown*. Garden City, N.Y.: Doubleday and Co., Inc., 1957.

McDowell, E. A., *Son of Man and Suffering Servant*. Nashville: Broadman, 1944.

Whale, J. S., *Victor and Victim*. Cambridge: The University Press, 1960.

8. Some ancient manuscripts omit this sentence. See footnote on p. 181 in *Gospel Parallels,* Revised Standard Version, New York: Thomas Nelson and Sons, 1949.

9. Of the many books written on the resurrection I mention:
Filson, Floyd, *Jesus Christ the Risen Lord*. New York: Abingdon Press, 1956.

Frost, Eric G., *This Jesus*. Great Neck, L. I., N.Y.: Channel Press, 1959.

Marney, Carlyle, *Faith in Conflict*. New York: Abingdon Press, 1957.

Near the close of this book, p. 151. Marney says:
"Even the Christ had to faith his way through death. Who would refuse to die for the sins of the world if he knew he would rise? He faithed his way; he pulled no rank on us! The heresy of our time is not that we preach Christ as if he were not God; it is rather that we preach Jesus as if he were not man. He faithed that the purpose of God would bring him through, and the Christian faith hangs on what the Father did! We have to faith it too."

10. Thus Filson begins Chapter II of *Jesus Christ The Risen Lord* referred to above.

11. John 20:19, 21 and 26.

VI. Peace and Salvation

In all Paul's epistles and in other New Testament letters, there is the salutation of "grace and peace." Quite often in the added phrase "from God our Father and the Lord Jesus Christ" we are reminded of the source of grace and peace. It is inescapable that peace has soteriological content. The message is the "good news of peace" (Eph. 6:15).

The early chapters of Romans set forth Paul's view of mankind without Christ. He paints a dark picture: pagan and Jew alike are lost and alienated from God. Man is enslaved to sin. He is at odds with himself and has enmity towards God. Through Christ God does for man what he cannot do for himself.

Peace With God

"Redemption" pictures emancipation from sin's slavery. "Forgiveness" pictures the canceling of a hopeless debt. "Justification" pictures acquittal at God's judgment bar and the provision for man of righteousness as God's gift through faith. "Adoption" pictures one who was an alien and far away from God being received as a son. "Expiation" pictures the removal of man's guilt through what Christ has done for him. "Reconciliation" portrays man as he is changed from an enemy to a friend of God. Hostility is replaced by peace and an open relation of fellowship. Man is reconciled. God is the reconciler.[1]

Although reconciliation is entirely God's work, its accomplishment depends upon man's acceptance of it. This acceptance is a matter of faith. The peace of reconciliation is, therefore, not to be thought of as a mere formal declaration of peace, or cessation of hostilities, but as a warm, vital relationship, characterized by a hearty acceptance in faith of what God through Christ has done for us.

We are to enjoy this peace with God, and yet Paul often relates suffering to discipleship, as for example in Romans 5:3-5: "More than that, we rejoice in our sufferings, knowing that suffering produces endurance, and endurance produces character, and character produces hope, and hope does not disappoint us, because God's love has been poured into our hearts through the Holy Spirit which has been given to us." As was already noted in Chapter V, the challenge to be willing to suffer is implicit in Jesus' understanding of peace.

Peace Among Men

In Ephesians 2:13-18 the thought of reconciliation carries with it the implication of breaking down the dividing wall of hostility between man and man. Frank Stagg[2] calls attention to the fact that the Book of Acts ends with an adverb — "unhinderedly." He says the purpose of Acts is "to show a victory of Christianity — to show the expansion of a concept, the liberation of the Gospel as it breaks through barriers that are religious, racial and national." There has never been a time in the history of the world when the breaking down of barriers was more needed.

Carlyle Marney[3] describes prejudice, that great creator of barriers:

> And what is prejudice? It is a vicious kind of mental slant pushed up out of your culture that makes up your mind for you before you think. It is an evil kind of mental blind spot that shuts from your view the facts of a given situation. It is a tyrannous mental fence that holds you from friendships you need and confines you to your own backyard. It may be racial,

religious, sectional, economic, or social. It is always personal, and in some sense it is always cultural. It is a symptom of pride, ignorance, and ego anywhere it happens to you, and it cuts across justice, perverts truth, subsists on lies, and worse; it twists and wastes personality, for whose sake culture exists to begin with.

We need to be reminded that "he is our peace," that he "has made us both one, and has broken down the dividing wall of hostility" (Eph. 2:14).

The positive note is the call to unity which is so central a theme in Ephesians and so much a part of the concept of peace. Christians are challenged to forbear one another in love and be "eager to maintain the unity of the Spirit in the bond of peace" (Eph. 4:3). This concept is reinforced in Colossians 3:15: "And the peace of Christ rule in your hearts, to which indeed you were called in the one body. . . ." This is a unity given, it is God's gift. We can fall short of it, we can hinder it, or we can surrender ourselves to be a part of the unity which is in Christ.

The Church for a time had peace from persecution (Acts 9:31), but it was not always that way. Sometimes the peace within the fellowship was threatened when people were selfish and hypocritical, as with Ananias and Sapphira (Acts 5), or domineering, as with Diotrephes (III John).

While still admitting it was not easy, Paul called men to their true relationship in Christ with such words as, "If possible, so far as it depends upon you, live peaceably with all" (Rom. 12:18). Towards those who are hostile there should be a will for unity expressing itself in prayer, benevolence, suffering and love. There is warmth and an outgoing quality to the concept of peace.[4]

Paul felt that a Christian wife or husband might be able to win an unbelieving mate to the Christian way (I Cor. 7: 12-14 and 16), but he was also open to the possibility that the unbelieving partner might desire to separate: ". . . let it be so; in such a case the brother or sisiter is not bound.

For God has called us to peace" (I Cor. 7:15). This, in-
cidentally, is one of the places where Paul is giving his own
judgment in this matter (I Cor. 7:12). There is, however,
a valid principle here that applies in relationships within and
outside marriage — peace may in some cases be found by
separation, and the separation need not be of a permanent
nature.

Peace is definitely connected with the idea of *koinonia* in
the New Testament. Frank Stagg[5] wonders if the Church in
modern times has ever even approximated what the Lord's
Supper meant to early Christians. We need more than anything this sense of fellowship, of sharing in the good things
and also in the suffering of Christ. So many forces would
pull us apart; we need the ties of love that bring us together.
There is a dynamic quality about peace just as there is about
koinonia. Peace as God's spiritual gift is like a warm flow
in which there is movement and power. It describes living
in a special way in which there is growth and sharing. Salvation in the New Testament is received and preserved in
community. Peace is one of the qualities of this life in community; it is one of the fruits of salvation; it is also one of
the picture words by which we describe salvation.

The power to realize community and individual peace does
not lie in the faithful themselves. This is the work of the
Father who is the giver of peace. Christians on their part
receive God's gift and become "peace-makers."

Inner Peace

Inner peace is another aspect of the relation of peace to
salvation. The clearest illustration of this is in Paul's mature
word to the Philippians (4:12) in which he tells them how
he has *learned* "how to be abased" and "how to abound," he
had "*learned* the secret of facing plenty and hunger, abun-
dance and want." The secret is his being "in Christ" who
gives him strength (4:13). It is in this setting and while a

prisoner that Paul speaks of this deep inner peace: "And the peace of God, which passeth all understanding shall guard your hearts and your thoughts in Christ Jesus" (Phil. 4:7 ASV).[6]

Wholeness, Welfare, and Well-Being

The idea of welfare, wholeness, and well-being with its rich preparation in the Old Testament is still another aspect of peace and its connection with salvation. Jesus came to make men whole — "Wilt thou be made whole?" (John 5: 6 KJV). J. B. Phillips wrote an entire book on this subject.[7]

A man lacking wholeness may be a schizophrenic — having a split mind. He may be paranoic — a mind alongside itself. He may be distracted — drawn in opposite directions. One without wholeness lacks integrity. He is not an integer. He may go "all to pieces."

> A severed hand
> Is an ugly thing, and man dissevered from the earth and stars and his history . . .
> Often appears atrociously ugly. Integrity is wholeness, the greatest beauty is
> Organic wholeness, the wholeness of life and things, the divine beauty of the universe.[8]

In the work of healing and helping men to be whole, faith, medicine, and psychiatry can combine as a team. Man needs to find One around whom the whole is integrated. The Christian message is that Christ is this One in whom and through whom all things hold together and find significance.[9] Purpose and meaning for life are found through sharing in His purpose and His love.

The Church ought to be the fellowship where men are being made whole. Purpose is found in helping one another through God's grace to be whole. Salvation is entering on a journey; we are on the way, with God's help, to becoming the person we each have the potential to become. Wholeness includes a concern for the welfare and wholeness of others, for in mutual concern is mutual uplift.

Wholeness and well-being are deeper than mere physical health. Paul carried with him his "thorn in the flesh." God did not remove it, but God gave him more grace (II Cor. 12:7-9). A person may be made whole and not physically cured. A life may possess a radiant joy and experience a unification of self while the body remains unhealed. Even death can be a form of healing in the fullness of faith.[10]

Ethical Connotations

There are ethical connotations to the idea of peace. Paul can say, "May the God of peace himself sanctify you wholly" (I Thess. 5:23a). There will be "glory and honor and peace for every one who does good" (Rom. 2:10a). "To set the mind on the flesh is death, but to set the mind on the Spirit is life and peace" (Rom. 8:6). "For the kingdom of God does not mean food and drink but righteousness and peace and joy in the Holy Spirit; he who thus serves Christ is acceptable to God and approved by men. Let us then pursue what makes for peace and for mutual upbuilding" (Rom. 14:17-19). "So shun youthful passions and aim at righteousness, faith, love and peace" (II Tim. 2:22a). You are not to say to someone, "Go in peace, be warmed and filled," and give him nothing (James 2:16). "But the wisdom from above is first pure, then peaceable, gentle, open to reason, full of mercy and good fruits, without uncertainty or insincerity. And the harvest of righteousness is sown in peace by those who make peace" (James 3:17-18).

Peace is listed more than once as one of the fruits of the Spirit (Gal. 5:22, et al.). A person does not pursue peace in order to realize salvation. The gift of peace is a fruit of God's gift of salvation. Peace in all of its interconnections becomes for the Christian a part of his life and outlook. It penetrates all relationships.

Cosmic Connotations

To say that peace has cosmic significance means that more than this planet earth is involved. For example, "Then the God of peace will soon crush Satan under your feet . . ." (Rom. 16:20). There is the note of eventual triumph over "principalities and powers" (Col. 2:15; Eph. 3:10; Phil. 2: 9-11). This belief takes on apocalyptic overtones in Revelation. The evil persecuting power of Rome with its requirement to worship the emperor is doomed. The Beast and the False Prophet are utterly defeated. There is temporary and then permanent defeat for Satan. There is defeat for the enigmatic Gog and Magog. The final note is one of victory and peace.

Peace is the present possession of the Christian. There is the tension in which we hold this peace, which is the subject of the next chapter. There is the goal out beyond this life where the process of becoming and the fullness of life finds continuance. There is the portrait of a beautiful City coming from God. There are new heavens and a new earth. All things are new. This is certainly related to the ultimate goal of peace.

NOTES

1. Rom 3:22-26 and 5:1, 2, 10. Peace linked with reconciliation is also seen in Col. 1:19-22. Here is shown clearly that the Father purposed the reconciling work of the Son and delighted in it. The cosmic aspects of Christ's work of reconciliation are intimated. Ketchum, *op. cit.,* pp. 25-48 is a whole chapter on "The Peace of Reconciliation" in which the exegetical details are expounded.
2. Stagg, Frank, *The Book of Acts.* Nashville, Tenn.: Broadman Press, 1955, p. 12.
3. Marney, Carlyle, *Faith in Conflict.* New York: Abingdon Press, 1957, p. 87. Marney's third chapter, "Faith and the Falcon" is a devastatingly real portrait of our culture and how we are conditioned by it. The picture is enlarged in Marney's, *Structures of Prejudice.* New York: Abingdon Press, 1961.
4. Other passages relating to this are: I Thess. 5:13; II Cor. 13:11; Phil. 4:2-3; and Rom. 14:33.

5. Stagg, Frank, *New Testament Theology*. Nashville, Tenn.: Broadman Press, 1962, chapter on the Lord's Supper.

6. Lightfoot, J. B., *St. Paul's Epistle to the Philippians,* Third edition. London: Macmillan and Co., 1873, pp. 268-331. In this famous discussion of "St. Paul and Seneca" Lightfoot considers at length the possible connections between these two men and between Stoicism and Christianity.

    Stoicism is a pantheistic religion of despair. It is hard to see any real positive help that Paul or anyone got from Stoicism, particularly with reference to the deep meaning of peace. This conclusion is supported by James S. Stewart's treatment of Stoicism in, *A Man in Christ*. New York: Harper and Bros., pp. 56-63.

7. Phillips, J. B., *Making Men Whole*. New York: Macmillan Co., 1953.

8. Magee, John, *Reality and Prayer*. New York: Harper and Bros., 1957, p. 122, he quotes the poet, Robinson Jeffers.

9. Colossians 1:17.

10. We are reminded of the cemetery inscriptions of early Christians, "In Peace" referred to at the end of Chapter IV.

VII. Peace in Tension

We have seen that the concept of peace is related to that which is most basic in the Christian faith: salvation in its manifold aspects, the cross, *agape,* and the struggle with evil.

In Germany prior to World War II a huge church had stood where God had been worshiped since the days of the Saxons, but in three days and nights of saturation bombing the church was obliterated. Even the trees in the churchyard were blown down. When the war ended, the people came creeping out of their hovels and began immediately to rebuild a house of worship. They could afford only a bare rectangular structure. However, an eccentric genius from the Rhineland provided some woodcarvings. He used the wood of the trees that had been blown down and carved twelve apostles and a heroic statue of Christ. This Christ, with its imperfections, rivets one's attention. Shrapnel protrudes from the shoulder, steel is visible in Christ's side, and His kneecap is broken. The woodcarver had made no attempt to remove bomb fragments that had lodged in the wood of the tree. Perhaps he was saying that here the message of the cross finds new expression, and Christ, by taking this all unto Himself, is showing us anew the true way to victory over hate and hostility.[1]

Tension and paradox are inescapable for the Christian. Both in searching out truth and in the endeavor to put truth into action there is the element of strain. If you stretch a spring it comes nearer to performing its function than if it never has any pull. Of course, a spring can be stretched until it snaps. It takes strain and tension for a locomotive to pull a train of cars. Too severe and sudden a pull may break a coupling. We have seen how Jesus anticipated this tension when He said, "Do not think that I have come to bring peace, but a sword."[2]

As Christians we are on the way to coming to know more about the peace of God and its manifold connections. We want more and more for God's gift of peace to affect our relationship to God and to our fellow men. This involves *agape* — loving with the love of God. Such love has no limits or arbitrary boundaries. Race, poverty, filth, degradation and hostility should not get in the way so far as we are concerned. If such barriers bar the way on the part of others, we should remain open and hopeful in our willingness to love. Such love has regard for the person as a person; it helps one who is not a person to become one. Such love wants, prays and works for the best in the person loved. Love like this will help the person become a better person. There is also a reflective benefit — it helps the one who loves to know himself better and to be more like the person God wants him to be.

One fruit of this love is the ability to accept another and in return to find acceptance. Acceptance means you remain open to a person. You come to know what seem to be his weaknesses and his shortcomings as well as his strong points, and you accept him as he is, or as he seems to be. Acceptance involves suspending judgment and the willingness to overlook weaknesses, looking for and hoping for the best. It means the willingness to give something of yourself, the willingness to listen, to take time, to share. This is not easy. Some of us are not very good at accepting ourselves. We fool ourselves; we downgrade ourselves; we condemn ourselves; we think too highly of ourselves; we do not really know ourselves. Well along in life, Willy Loman in *Death of a Salesman*[3] says, "I still feel — kind of temporary about myself." After his death, his son Biff says of him, "He never knew who he was." Actually, the best way to come to know oneself better is in the fellowship of coming to know another. As we accept him with his weaknesses, we are able to face up to our own. As we look for, hope for and work for something better in him, it brings out that which is better in us. The basis for acceptance is that God accepts us. He knows us far better than we know ourselves. He loves us with an uplifting love, and this makes for peace in its fullest spiritual sense.

C. S. Lewis[4] says we can love people we do not like when we love with God's kind of love, and if we love them long enough, we may even come to like them, and they may become more likeable. He reminds us that we do not always like ourselves, but we keep on loving ourselves.

Martin Buber[5] is expanding the same truth when he speaks of the I-Thou relationship as becoming reciprocal and mutually upbuilding. Yet Buber also soberly reminds us that we do not always stay on this lofty plane of I-Thou. We descend to I-it, to using another person and treating him as a thing. The tension is there, even when we have these high moments of person-to-person sharing in love.

Peace in tension stands in close relationship to the meaning of the cross. Recently a novel interpretation of the "legions of angels"[6] on whom Jesus might have called has been offered, with the suggestion that Jesus was all too keenly aware of the revolutionary forces available with which He might align Himself. Whether this is exegetically legitimate is open to question, but it is thought-provoking. Anyway, Jesus did *not* call on them! He did not come down from the cross. He did not vilify those who put Him there. Rather, He prayed for their forgiveness.

When Jesus tried to prepare His disciples for the cross, they did not understand.[7] Related to this fact is the idea of the first being last and above all, the willingness to be a servant. It was hard for the disciples to grasp this idea. It still is for us today, and herein lies tension. In the events leading up to the cross and on the cross itself, Jesus responded to enmity and hostility with love. In this way He broke the vicious circle that always builds up: hate, malice, vengeance, retaliation. His word to us is "take up your cross and follow me," and herein lies tension, because we do not want to be pulled apart on a cross; we do not want to suffer; we do not even want to be a servant.

This is not meant to say that to prove you are a Christian you must self-consciously seek a way to suffer with a sort of martyr complex. There is even an abject way of trying to be a servant that is actually an insult.

However, even when we are closest to following Jesus we must confess how little there is in it of a cross, and of serving, and how very difficult it is to love with God's love.

But now and then when we have some little glimpse of this truth in our own experience, we see there is tension of another kind. For those who do not have it often resent it when they see it in another. But there can be the positive response too, as with the Centurion — "Truly this was a son of God" (Matt. 27:54).

Sometime, in some situation of strain, someone may be impressed to observe of some action or word of yours that you were "a Christian," and if this means that you at that moment acted like Christ, you have known and borne witness to God's gift of peace and love.

What bearing does God's peace have on our need for peace in this nuclear age? Its relationship to the living of the Christian life should already be apparent: we are on the way, we are in the process of becoming God's sons. God's love, the way of the cross, the willingness to serve provide the center around which life finds meaning and purpose in person-to-person relationships.

The Greeks fashioned the concept of a just war, the object of which was to vindicate justice and restore peace, in which violence should be minimal. Plato protested against the ruining of wells and orchards and made a distinction among the enemy between the innocent and the guilty.[8] The Cluny movement which began in 910 took an interest in the "just war" from the viewpoint of restraints on the fighting of a war. For example, with the Truce of God the times of fighting were restricted, stipulating no fighting from sunset Wednesday to Monday morning. The Peace of God restricted the range of the combatants. There were to be no attacks upon priests, nuns, or pilgrims, or upon merchants or farmers, their animals, tools, or properties.[9] This led to further development of rules for warfare which included treatment of prisoners, respect for ambassadors, and suppression of private reprisals.[10] Eventually this development of just methods of fighting wars culminated in the principles of the Geneva Convention.

So far as Christian attitudes toward participation in war, for the most part there was pacifism until the time of Constantine.[11] Augustine said that war should only be conducted under the auspices of the State, because private war is anarchy.[12] Thus in the fourth and fifth centuries the concept of a just war predominated. The object was to vindicate justice and restore peace. Christians fought under the authority of the State. They sought to observe a code of good faith and humanity. Augustine added that the motive must be love and that monks and priests were exempted. The next attitude toward war was the crusade. In this case the enemy was on the outside and the code tended to break down. Pacifism has usually been associated with withdrawal. The way called for qualified participation. The Crusade emphasized the dominance of the church over the world. In the Middle Ages pacifism was represented by the sects. In the Renaissance, there was just war in Italy among the city states. Among the humanists, there was extensive propaganda for peace on the basis of a Christian, humanist culture. The Reformation precipitated wars of religion.[13] In World War I the churches of the United States took a crusading attitude. With World War II it was again the idea of a just war. The atomic bomb has brought bewilderment and division. The pacifism emerging is not based primarily on Christian principles, but simply on the desire for survival.

It is hard to see how any Christian could want a thermonuclear war. Herman Kahn in his monumental study, *On Thermonuclear War*,[14] contends that many regard thermonuclear war as "unthinkable," and by this they mean they do not want to think about it. He holds that by considering the horrifying eventualities of total war and by preparing for them, they become less possible. People ought to read this brilliant scientific analysis of a complex problem, whether they agree with his suggestions or not. In the opening lines of his Preface Kahn says:

> Men and governments have long lived with the painful problem of choice. Even those with courage to make hard choices and the willingness to choose resolutely between good and evil, redemption and damnation, joy and sorrow, have never been able to insure the final result. The final outcome of benevolent, informed and intelligent decisions may turn out to be disastrous. But the choices must be made; dies must be cast. So it is with the most dramatic choices open to the free world in our day: arms control, peaceful coexistence, rearmament, dynamic rollback, appeasement, Soviet domination, thermonuclear war, or whatever shifting alternatives seem most appealing or least palatable from year to year.[15]

Then at the close of the Preface he says:

> I have a firm belief that unless we have more serious and sober thought on various facets of the strategic problem than seems to be typical of most discussions today, both classified and unclassified, we are not going to reach the year 2000, and maybe not even 1965, without a cataclysm of some sort, and that this cataclysm will prove a lot more cataclysmic than it needs to be.[16]

We are now past 1965, but there is still uneasiness about reaching the twenty-first century.

Kahn refers to Neville Shute's *On the Beach* as "interesting but badly researched." He says we do not have to suppose total extinction. However, he goes on to say that thermo-nuclear war will quite likely be an unprecedented catas-trophe for the defender. It may, or may not be, for the at-tacker and for certain neutrals.[17] "Unprecedented" does not mean "unlimited." The limits on the magnitude of the catastrophe seem to be closely dependent on what kind of preparations have been made, and on how the war is started and fought. Though some people scoff at attempts to reduce casualties from 100 million to 50 million, he has tables to show what kind of recuperation might be expected in a variety of circumstances. He asks such questions as "Will the survivors envy the dead?"[18] He gives this sequence in a fatal dose of radiation: First you become nauseated, then sick; you seem to recover, then in two or three weeks you really get sick and die. He speaks of the need for radiation meters. Vomiting spreads psychologically. Many will think they have an overdose of radiation when they have not. You look at a man's meter and say, "You've only received ten roentgens, why are you vomiting? Pull yourself together and get to work."[19]

It seemed necessary to inject this much of the reality of the problem facing us today as it may relate to the present-day relevance of the biblical concept of peace. There are numer-ous other sources that wrestle with this problem in a variety of ways.

A summary of Bainton's outlook is helpful at this point: The development of technology and the dehumanizing of war have progressively excluded middle courses and nar-rowed the range of choice. Two colossi now face each other, each possessed of the power to paralyze the other, if not to liquidate the globe. Against nuclear destruction there is no military defense.[20] Human life is good, yet the survival of man is neither to be despised nor to be inordinately cher-ished. To be Christian, an ethic must posit and seek to implement in proper balance: love, justice, the integrity of the self and the integrity of the other person, even should he be the enemy.[21]

Bainton himself takes the position of pacifism. He says that there is a Christian pacifism of renunciation and a secularist pacifism of prudence. Christian pacifism is not a strategy but a witness. Conscientious objectors have never been numerous enough to stop a war.

What then? Bainton asks, and tries to answer. The pacifist must dissociate himself from war. He need not therefore dissociate himself from all political life. The Quakers have not done so. Pacifists agitate for legislation looking toward the elimination or mitigation of war.[22] At present there is more need for peace than there is for pacifism. If peace is preserved it will be through the efforts not of pacifists, but of peace-minded non-pacifists who do not renounce war absolutely, but who oppose war in our time on grounds of humanitarianism and the pragmatic.[23] Perhaps this is where "Blessed are the peace makers" is best understood. Peacemaking is positive and not the neutrality of pacifism.

From Bainton and others come some practical suggestions. Some of them are long-range. The hope of attaining some may seem remote. Tension in the biblical concept of peace has already been admitted, but there is a challenge and an inspiration and a hope here too. The desire for peace is universal; less so, the will to peace. It seems to me that the Christian is called to lend his influence toward the will to peace: peace among men, peace of man with God, and peace among nations. Kahn[24] says, "It is the hallmark of the amateur and the dilettante that he had almost no interest in how to get to his particular Utopia. Perhaps this is because the practical job of finding a path may be more difficult than the job of designing the goal."

Christians, in living and bearing witness to the total message of the Gospel, can by their faithfulness influence the total will to peace. Peace is not the achievement of man; it is God's gift. In its fullest sense peace may not be attainable in this life or on this earth. Yet, there can be peace in the midst of tension, and the Christian ought to lend his influence to practical measures for encouraging peace among men. In helping men to a right relationship with God the way is opened for God's gift of peace to be realized, for we are responsible, individually and collectively, for the choices to be made and the life to be lived in our day.

When Dante was exiled from his home in Florence he determined to walk from Italy to Paris where he could study philosophy in an effort to find the real meaning of life. He came late at night to the gates of a Franciscan monastery at Lunigiana and was asked by the friar who opened the door, "What do you wish?" Dante answered with one word:

"Peace."[25]

Marcus Barth[26] in summing up his study of Ephesians closes with words so appropriate that I use them as a concluding postscript:

> This peace which was preached by Christ himself (Eph. 2:17) is a political and social event of unlimited dimensions. Such peace, when we consider its breadth, length, height, and depth, surpasses all understanding (3:18 f.), not by its being limited to another world or to man's inner life only, but because it was 'made' (2:14 f.) in this world and for this world. Therefore it reaches into the divided soul of both ancient and modern man. It concerns and forbids the crime of preparation for an atomic war. It unmasks and fights the creeping threat of anti-Semitism. It throws burning light into the entangled problems of ecumenical unity and mission work. In short, it is inexhaustible; and yet we are made to know of it and make it known! Christians who are desirous of learning more about it will gain understanding, inasmuch as they actually live in faith and serve God in their daily lives; i.e., when they dare to show that they boldly trust in the validity of God's work and message. They need not be afraid of being too confident, too hopeful, or too daring, for God himself and the Gospel itself are for all men everywhere,

and at every time. According to this Gospel, through Jesus
Christ and the Spirit, God himself does away with all the dividing walls and enmities. In this faith, Christians can stand firm
and can grow together. They have beneath them a solid ground,
and they have shoes that bear them securely. Therefore (Eph.
5:14),

> 'Stand up, O sleeper,
> And arise from the dead,
> And Christ will give you light!'

NOTES

1. Paraphrased and adapted from James K. McCord's, "The Peace
   of God" in *And Our Defense is Sure,* edited by Harmon D.
   Moore, Ernest A. Ham and Clarence E. Hobgood. Nashville,
   Tenn: Abingdon Press, 1964, pp. 48-49.
2. Buttrick and others, editors, *The Interpreter's Bible.* Nashville,
   Tenn.: Abingdon Press, 1951, Vol. 7, p. 373.
3. Miller, Arthur, *Death of a Salesman.* New York: The Viking
   Press, 1950, p. 51 and p. 138.
4. Lewis, C. S., *Mere Christianity.* Glasgow: Collins Press, Fontana Books, 1955, pp. 102 ff. and 113-115.
5. Buber, Martin, *I and Thou.* Edinburgh: T.& T. Clark, 1953.
6. Matthew 26:53. On this see Dix, Dom Gregory, *Jew and Greek.*
   London: Dacre Press, A. & C. Black, Ltd., 1953, reprinted
   1955, p. 21.
7. Mark 8:31-33 and 9:30-32.
8. Bainton, Roland H., *Christendom,* Vol. 1. New York: Harper
   and Row, Harper (Torchbooks) 131, 1966, pp. 19-20.
9. *Ibid.,* pp. 168 ff. and 178.
10. *Ibid.,* p. 249.
11. Bainton, Roland H., *Christian Attitudes Toward War and Peace*:
    A Historical Survey and Critical Re-evaluation. Nashville, Tenn.:
    Abingdon Press, 1960. In this connection Bainton says, p. 53,
    "Prior to Christianity there is no record of anyone suffering
    death for a refusal of military service. Until the time of Con-
    stantine no extant Christian writing countenanced Christian par-
    ticipation in war. The attitude of the Gospels toward a soldier's
    calling is neutral. The pacifism in the New Testament is not
    from a New Testament legalism, but from an effort to apply
    what was taken to be the mind of Christ."
12. *Ibid.,* p. 164.
13. *Ibid.,* p. 150 . . . In the time of Cromwell the *Soldier's Pocket
    Bible* compiled by Edmund Calamy in 1643 manfully disposed of
    the Sermon on the Mount by placing together the following

verses: Matt. 5:44, "But I say unto you, love your enemies." and II Chron. 19:2, "Would'st thou help the wicked and love them that hate the Lord?" and Psalm 139:21-22, "Do not I hate them, O Lord, that hate thee? . . . I hate them with an unfeigned hatred, as they are mine utter enemies." The summary is that the soldier must "love his enemies as they are his enemies, and hate them as they are God's enemies."

14. Kahn, Herman, *On Thermonuclear War*. Princeton, N.J.: Princeton University Press, 1960.
15. *Ibid.,* Preface.
16. *Loc. cit.*
17. *Ibid.,* p. 10.
18. *Ibid.,* p. 20.
19. *Ibid.,* p. 86.
20. Bainton, *op. cit.,* p. 230.
21. *Ibid.,* pp. 239-242.
22. *Ibid.,* p. 252.
23. *Ibid.,* p. 253. This statement is especially interesting coming from a pacifist.
24. Kahn, *op. cit.,* p. 7.
25. I am indebted in part for the details of this familiar story of Dante to McCord, *op. cit.,* p. 44, see note 1 above. Part of the details I read in another source which I am unable to trace.
26. Barth, Marcus, *The Broken Wall*. Philadelphia: The Judson Press, 1959, pp. 266-267.

Bibliography

Albright, W. F., "The Hebrew Expression for 'Making a Covenant' in Pre-Israelite Documents," *The Bulletin of American Schools of Oriental Research,* New Haven, Conn., 1951.

Arndt. W. F., and F. W. Gingrich, *A Greek-English Lexicon of the New Testament and Other Early Christian Literature.* Chicago: University of Chicago Press, 1957.

Baehr, Karl, editor, *Land Reborn.* New York: American Christian Palestine Committee, Sept.-Oct., 1958 and May, 1961.

Bainton, Roland H., *Christendom,* Vol. 1, Harper (Torchbooks) 131. New York: Harper and Row, 1966, 274 pp.

Bainton, Roland H., *Christian Attitudes Toward War and Peace: A Historical Survey and Critical Re-evaluation.* New York: Abingdon Press, 1960, 299 pp.

Barr, John S., "The Christian Church and Peace," *Chinese* Rec., Dec., 1934.

Barth, Marcus, *The Broken Wall.* Philadelphia: Judson Press, 1959, 272 pp.

Bender, Harold S., "The Pacifism of the Sixteenth Century Anabaptists," reprinted from *Church History,* XXIV:2, June, 1955.

Berdyaev, Nicolas, *The Realm of Spirit and the Realm of Caesar.* Translated by Donald A. Lowrie. New York: Harper and Bros., 1952, 182 pp.

Buber, Martin, *I and Thou.* Edinburgh: T. & T. Clark, 1953, 120 pp.

Bunche, Ralph, "Some Reflections on Peace in Our Time," (A Lecture delivered on the occasion of his receipt of the Nobel Peace Prize), *Norseman,* Jan., 1951.

Burton, E. D., *A Critical and Exegetical Commentary on the Epistle to the Galatians* (ICC). New York: Charles Scribner's Sons, 1928, 541 pp.

Butterfield, H., *Christianity and History.* London: G. Bell and Sons, Ltd., 1954, 146 pp.

Buttrick, G. A., and others, editors, *The Interpreter's Bible,* 12 vols. New York: Abingdon Press, 1952-57.

Caspari, *Vorstellung und Wort 'Friede' im Alten Testament.*

Charles, R. H., *Religious Development Between the Old and New Testaments.* London: Oxford University Press, first published 1914, reprinted to at least 1945, 256 pp.

Chesterton, G. K., "Peace and Pacifism," *Saturday Review,* Oct. 1934.

Condenhove-Kalergi, Richard, *From War to Peace.* Translated by Constantine Fitzgibbon, London: Jonathan Cape, 1959, 224 pp.

Copleston, F. C., "Pacifism and the New Testament," *Church Quarterly Review,* Oct., 1937.

Cornbach, Abraham, *The Jewish Peace Book for Home and School.* Cincinnati, Ohio: Department of Synagogue and School Extension of the Union of Hebrew Congregations, 1932.

————————, *The Quest For Peace.* Cincinnati, Ohio: Sinai Press, 1937.

Davis, G. M., "Opinion Concerning the Pacifism of Jesus," *The Journal of Bible and Religion,* July 1949.

David, H. F., "The Early Christian Attitude to War," *Blackfriars,* Oct. 1949.

Davis, Jerome, *Peace, War and You.* West Haven, Conn.: Promoting Enduring Peace, Inc.

————, *Religion in Action.* New York: Philosophical Library, Inc.

Denney, James, *The Death of Christ.* London: Hodder & Stoughton, 1902, 334 pp.

Dodd, C. H., *The Bible and the Greeks.* London: Hodder & Stoughton, 1935, 264 pp.

Eichrodt. Walther, "Friede," in *Die Religion im Geschichte und Gegenwart,* Second Edition, Tubingen: J. C. B. Mohr; Gunkel and others, editors, 1928.

————————, "Die Hoffnung des ewigen Friedens im Alten Israel," B F Th 25, 3(1920).

Filson, Floyd V., *Jesus Christ the Risen Lord.* New York: Abingdon Press, 1956, 288 pp.

Flanders, H. J., Robert Crapps and David Smith, *People of the Covenant.* New York: The Ronald Press Co., 1963, 479 pp.

Fleming, James, "Is there Pacifism in the Old Testament?" *Anglican Theological Review,* Jan. 1929.

Friedrich, C. J., *Inevitable Peace.* Boston: Harvard University Press, 1948, 294 pp.

Frost, Eric G., *This Jesus.* Great Neck, L. I., N.Y.: Channel Press, 1959, 132 pp.

Fuchs, H., "Augustin und der antike Friedensgedanke," N Ph U 3 (1926) 39-43; 167-223.

Gesenius, William, *Hebrew and Chaldee Lexicon to the Old Testament Scriptures.* With additions and corrections from the author's *Thesaurus* and other works, by Samuel Prideaux Tregelles, 1867, 884 pp.

——————, *A Hebrew and English Lexicon of the Old Testament.* Based on the lexicon of Gesenius as translated by Edward Robinson, edited with constant reference to the *Thesaurus* of Gesenius as completed by E. Rödiger, and with authorized use of the latest German editions of Gesenius' *Handwörterbuch über das Alte Testament* by Francis Brown with the cooperation of S. H. Driver and Charles A. Briggs. Oxford: Clarendon Press, 1906.

Glueck, Nelson, *Hesed in the Bible.* Translated by Alfred Gottschalk. Cincinnati, Ohio: The Hebrew Union College Press, 1967, 107 pp.

Green, Thomas F., "The Basis of Christian Pacifism," *Friends Quarterly,* April, 1952.

Green, William C., "Some Ancient (Greek and Roman) Attitudes Towards War and Peace," *Classical Journal,* June 1944.

Graham, William, *Peace With God.* Garden City, N.Y.: Doubleday and Co., 1953, 222 pp.

Haffner, Sebastian, "The Price of Peace," *World Review,* April, 1949.

Halifax, Viscount, "The Christian View of Peace," *Listener,* July 14, 1937.

Harnack, A., *Militia Christie.* Translated by J. Moffatt. New York: G. P. Putnam's Sons, 1904.

Hassler, Alfred, editor, *Fellowship.* Nyack, N.Y.: Fellowship of Reconciliation, Nov. 1, 1960.

Hatch, Edwin, *The Influence of Greek Ideas on Christianity.* New York: Harper (Torchbooks), 1957, 359 pp.

Hatch and Redpath, *A Concordance to the Septuagint.* Graz, Austria: Akademische Druck-V. Verlagsanstalt, 1954.

Headlan, A. D., "The Christian Attitude to the War and the Peace," *Quarterly Review,* Jan. 1945.

Hearnshaw, F. J. C., "Is Christianity Committed to Pacifism?" *Hibbert Journal,* Oct. 1940.

Heering, G. J., *The Fall of Christianity.* London: G. Allen and Unwin Bros., Ltd., 1930.

Herburg, Will, *The Writings of Martin Buber,* selected and edited by Will Herburg. Meridian Books, New York: World Publishing Co.

Hickey, Owen, "UNESCO and Peace," *Fortnightly,* Aug., 1950.

Houghton, Louise Seymour, *Hebrew Life and Thought.* Chicago: University of Chicago Press, 1906.

Hunter, A. M., *Design for Life.* London: SCM Press, Ltd., 1953, 124 pp.

Jacob, Edmond, *Theology of the Old Testament.* Translated by

Arthur W. Heathcote and Philip J. Allcock. New York: Harper and Bros., 1958, 368 pp.

Josephus, Flavius, *The Life .and Works of Flavius Josephus,* Translated by William Whiston. Philadelphia: The John C. Winston Co., 1055 pp.

Jolly, Isaac, *Pacifism at the Bar of Holy Scripture and History,* 1936.

Kahn, Herman, *On Thermonuclear War.* Princeton, N.J.: Princeton University Press, 1960, 651 pp.

Kant, Immanuel, *Perpetual Peace*: A Philosophical Essay. Translated by M. Campbell. London: Swan Sonnenschein and Co., 1903.

Ketchum, Henry Crady, *Eiphnh in the New Testament,* an unpublished Ph.D. thesis, The Southern Baptist Theological Seminary, Louisville, Ky., 1933, 140 pp.

Kittel, Gerhard, *Theologisches Wörterbuch Zum Neuen Testament.* Stuttgart: Verlag Von W. Kohlhammer, 1935.

Koehler, L., and W. Baumgartner, *Lexicon in Veteris Testamenti Libros.* Leiden: E. J. Brill, 1953, 1138 pp.

Köhler, Ludwig, *Old Testament Theology,* Translated by A. S. Todd. Philadelphia: The Westminster Press. (Lutterworth Press, 1957). Type set in G. B. Printed in U.S.A. This book originally appeared as *Theologie des Alten Testament,* Tübingen: J. C. B. Mohr, 1953. This translation has been made from the third revised edition, 1953.

Lawson, James G., editor, *Great Sermons on World Peace.* (The sermons are by: Edgar De Witt Jones, Rabbi Louis L. Mann, Agnes Maude Royden, Joseph Fort Newton, Harold Paul Sloan, William Temple, William P. Merrill, Harry E. Fosdick, William E. Biederwolf, Ernest Fremont Tittle, Francis J. McConnell, and George A. Oldham.) New York: Round Table Press, Inc., 1937.

Leivestad, Ragnar, *Christ the Conqueror*: Ideas of Conflict and Victory. London: S.P.C.K., 1954.

Lewis, C. S., *Mere Christianity.* Glasgow: Collins Press, Fontana Books, 1955, 188 pp.

Librorum Sacrorum Veteris Testamenti Concordantiae Hebraicae atque Chaldaicae. Ipsaiae: Julio Fuerstio, 1840.

Liebmann, J. L., *Peace of Mind.* New York: Simon and Schuster, 1946, 203 pp.

Lightfoot, J. B., *St. Paul's Epistle to the Philippians.* London: Macmillan and Co., 1873, 346 pp.

Lillie, "The Just War," *Expository Times,* April, 1952.

Mac Arthur, J. S., "The Pre-exilic Prophets and Pacifism," *Expository Times,* Dec. 1940.

Mac Gregor, G. H. C., "The Church and Peace," *Outlook,* April, 1936.

_____, *The New Testament Basis of Pacifism.* New York: Fellowship of Reconciliation, 1947.

Manson, William, *Jesus the Messiah.* Philadelphia: The Westminster Press, 1946, 267 pp.

Mackay, John A., *God's Order.* New York: Macmillan Co., 1953, 214 pp.

Marney, Carlyle, *Faith in Conflict.* New York: Abingdon Press, 1957, 158 pp.

_____, *Structures of Prejudice.* New York: Abingdon Press, 1961, 256 pp.

Maston, T. B., *Christianity and World Issues.* New York: Macmillan Co., 1957, 374 pp.

Mayor, N. E., "True Christian Teaching Applied to This War," *New Church Magazine,* Jan. 1940.

McCord, James I., "The Peace of God," in *And Our Defense is Sure,* edited by Harmon D. Moore, Ernest A. Ham and Clarence E. Hobgood. New York: Abingdon Press, 1964. Also: Edw. H. Pruden, "The Spiritual Basis for Peace."

McDowell, E. A., *Son of Man and Suffering Servant.* Nashville, Tenn.: Broadman Press, 1944, 216 pp.

McFadyen, John Edgar, *The Message of Israel.* London: James Clarke and Co., Ltd., 1931.

Miller, Arthur, *Death of a Salesman.* New York: The Viking Press, 1950, 139 pp.

More, Thomas, *Utopia.* Introduction by Mildred Campbell. New York: D. Van Nostrand Co., Inc., 1947, first published 1516.

Moulton, W. F. and A. S. Geden, *A Concordance to the Greek New Testament.* Edinburgh: T. & T. Clark, 1899.

Mowinkel, S., *He That Cometh.* Translated by G. W. Anderson. New York: Abingdon Press, 1954, 528 pp.

_____, *The Old Testament as Word of God.* Translated by Reidar B. Bjornard. New York: Abingdon Press, 1959, 144 pp.

Murray, Kenneth J., "How Christ Met Evil," an unpublished B. D. thesis, McGill University, March, 1954.

Niebuhr, R., *An Interpretation of Christian Ethics.* New York: Harper and Bros., 1935, 244 pp.

_____, "Critique of Pacifism," *Atlantic Monthly,* May, 1927.

Noth, Martin, *The History of Israel.* Translated by Stanley Godman, from second German edition. New York: Harper and Bros., 1958.

_____, "Das Alttestamentliche Bundschliessen Im Lichte Eines Mari-Textes," *Theologische Bucherei.* Munchen: Chr. Kaiser Verlag, 1955-57.

_____, "The Re-presentation of the Old Testament in Proclamation," *Interpretation,* XV:1, Jan. 1961.

Oehler, G. F., *Theology of the Old Testament.* Translated by George
    E. Day, second edition. New York: Funk and Wagnalls, 1884.

PAMPHLETS ON PEACE

"The Peacable Christian," A Sermon on Rom. 12:18, London, 1678,
    in New College Library, University of Edinburgh, B.a./6.5.
"Eiphnikon," or, A treatise on Peace, by Irenaeus Philadelphus,
    Philantrophos, London, 1660, in New College Library, University
    of Edinburgh, B.a./3/43.
"Peace and Truth," London, 1938, New College Library, University
    of Edinburgh, Zh 28.
"Peace and War," by Albert Schweitzer, 1954, New College Library,
    University of Edinburgh, Zn. 24.
"Peace or Atomic War," by Albert Schweitzer, three appeals broad-
    cast at Oslo, Norway, April 28, 29 and 30, 1958. New York:
    Holt and Co. In Vanderbilt University Library, 341.67 S41 P.
Peace Conference, Edinburgh, 1853, New College, University of
    Edinburgh, U.h. 12.
"Peace," Redpath, New College Library, University of Edinburgh,
    W.g.4. B.c./10.15.
Five Tracts Against War by Society for Promotion of Permanent
    and Universal Peace, 1817-1818, New College Library, University
    of Edinburgh, A.c./1.3.
"The Coming Peace," by the Committee on World Peace, J. M.
    Dawson, Chairman, Nashville, Tenn.: The Sunday School Board
    of the Southern Baptist Convention. (This little pamphlet lists the
    titles of a number of other books and pamphlets.)
"We Have Peace," Department of Evangelism, The American Bap-
    tist Home Mission Society, New York.
The following PAMPHLETS are published by The Fellowship of
    Reconciliation, London:
"The Fellowship of Reconciliation: Its Basis."
"Chung Chi's Red Pants."
Caird, George B., "War and the Christian."
Ferguson, John, "Letter to a Non-Pacifist," and "Would Christ Have
    Pressed the Button?"
Fosdick, H. E., "The Unknown Soldier."
Macgregor, G. H. C., "Looking to Our Foundations."
The following PAMPHLETS are published by Promoting Enduring
    Peace, Inc., West Haven, Conn.:
"Leaders of America on Russia."
Rabinowitch, Eugene, "Walking the Plank to Nowhere."
Stanfield, Boris, M., "Wanted: 'A Dynamic Foreign Policy.' "

Peace, Research For: Results of a Prize Contest, published for the
    Institute for Social Research, Oslo; published by North Holland

Publishing Co., Amsterdam, 1954, in Emory University Library, Atlanta, Ga., JX1952 R43.

Peace, The Book of: A Collection of Essays on War and Peace. Boston: George C. Beckwith, 1845, in Vanderbilt University Library, Nashville, Tenn., 341.1 C271.

Pedersen, Johs., Israel: *Its Life and Culture*. I-II & III-IV. London: Oxford University Press, I-II first published 1926, reprinted 1954, 578 pp.; III-IV first published 1940, reprinted 1953, 788 pp.

Penn, William, "An Essay Towards the Present and Future Peace of Europe By the Establishment of an European Diet, Parliament or Estates," in *International Conciliation Documents* for the year 1943. New York: Carnegie Endowment for International Peace, in Vanderbilt University Library, Nashville, Tenn., 172.4 I61 No. 394.

Porteous, Norman W., "SHALEM-SHALOM" Glasgow University Oriental Society Transactions, Vol. X, Years 1940-41 edited by C. J. Mullo Weir. Glasgow: Civic Press, Ltd., 1943, in New College Library, University of Edinburgh.

Phillips, J. B., *Making Men Whole*. New York: Macmillan Co., 1953, 73 pp.

Ramsey, Paul, *War and the Christian Conscience*. Durham, N. C.: Duke University Press, 1961, 331 pp.

Raven, C. E., *The Theological Basis of Christian Pacifism*. New York: The Fellowship of Reconciliation, 1950.

Revised Standard Version of the Bible. New York: Thomas Nelson and Sons, 1952.

Richardson, Alan, *A Theological Word Book of the Bible*. London: SCM Press, Ltd., 1950, 290 pp.

Robertson, A. T., *A Grammar of the Greek New Testament in the Light of Historical Research*, fifth edition. New York: Harper and Bros., first published 1914, fifth edition 1931, 1454 pp.

――――――, *Paul's Joy in Christ*. New York: Fleming H. Revell Co., 1917, 267 pp.

Rowley, H. H., *The Faith of Israel*. Philadelphia: The Westminster Press, 1956, 220 pp.

――――――, "Melchizedek and Zadok," in *Festschrift Alfred Bertholet*, Tübingen: J. C. B. Mohr, 1950.

――――――, *The Relevance of the Apocalyptic*. London: Lutterworth Press, 1952, 327 pp.

Rutenber, C. G., *The Dagger and the Cross*. New York: Fellowship Publications, 1952.

Schultz, Herman, *Old Testament Theology*. Translated from the fourth German edition by J. A. Patterson. Edinburgh: T. & T. Clark, 1898.

Scott, Ernest F., *The Ethical Teaching of Jesus*. New York: The Macmillan Co., 1951, 133 pp.

Septuagint Version of the Old Testament and Apocrypha with an English Translation. London: Samuel Bagster and Sons, Ltd.

Sheen, Fulton J., *Peace of Soul* London: Blantford Press, Ltd., 1950.

Slick, Tom, *Permanent Peace.* Englewood Cliffs, N.J.: Prentice-Hall, 1958, 181 pp.

Snaith, N. H., *Distinctive Ideas of the Old Testament.* Philadelphia: Westminster Press, 1947, 251 pp.

Somerville, John, *The Philosophy of Peace.* New York: Gaer Associates, 1949, 264 pp.

Stagg, Frank, *The Book of Acts.* Nashville, Tenn.: Broadman Press, 1955, 281 pp.

------------, *New Testament Theology.* Nashville, Tenn.: Broadman Press, 1962, 361 pp.

Stauffer, E., *Christ and the Caesars.* Translated by K. & R. Gregor Smith. Philadelphia: Westminster Press, 1955, 293 pp.

------------, *New Testament Theology.* Translated by John Marsh, London: SCM Press, Ltd., 1955, 373 pp.

Stevens, George B., *The Theology of the New Testament.* New York: Charles Scribner's Sons, 1914, 619 pp.

Stevens, Paul M., *The Ultimate Weapon of Christianity.* New York: Thomas Nelson and Sons, 1961, 158 pp.

Stewart, James S., *A Faith to Proclaim.* New York: Charles Scribner's Sons, 1953, 160 pp.

------------, *A Man in Christ.* New York: Harper and Bros., 1957, 332 pp.

Strausz-Hupe, Robert, "No Peace in Our Time," *The Officer,* Nov., 1958, Nashville, Tenn.: published by the Reserve Officers Association.

Strong, James, *The Exhaustive Concordance of the Bible.* London: Hodder and Stoughton, 1894.

Temple, S. A., Jr., "Anglican Statement on the Theology of Peace and War," *Anglican Theological Review,* April 1949.

Thayer, J. H., *A Greek-English Lexicon of the New Testament,* a translation and revision of Grimm and Wilke's *Clavis Novi Testamenti.* New York: American Book Co., 1889, copyright by Harper and Bros., 723 pp.

Tompkinson, Cyril, "The Ideal of Peace in the Bible," *Bookman,* Dec., 1931.

Van Leeuwen, W. S., EIRENE IN HET NIEUWE TESTAMENT. Wageningen: H. Veeman and Zonen, 1940.

Veteris Testamenti Concordantiae Hebraicae atque Chaldaicae. Lipsiae: Solomon Mandelkern, 1900.

von Rad, Gerhard, "Ancient Word and Living Word," *Interpretation,* XV:1, Jan., 1961.

------------, *Theologie des Alten Testaments,* Band I & II. Munchen: Chr. Kaiser Verlag, 1958 & 1960.

_____, *Moses.* New York: World Christian Book Association Press.

_____, "Typological Interpretation of the Old Testament," *Interpretation,* XV:2, April, 1961.

Weir, Ernest T., "Survey of the Road to Peace," an address given at a luncheon meeting of the Poor Richard Club, Philadelphia, March 13, 1956.

Wickramasinghe, "Christianity and Peace," Baptist Quarterly, Jan., 1950.

Wilder, A. P., *Eschatology and Ethics in the Teachings of Jesus.* New York: Harper and Bros., 1950.

Whale, J. S., *Victor and Victim.* Cambridge: The University Press, 1960, 172 pp.

Wheeler-Bennett, John W., *The Pipe Dream of Peace.* New York: William Morrow and Co., 1935.

White, Dorrance S., "The Attitude of the Romans Towards Peace and War," *Classical Journal,* May 1936.

Wolf, William J., *No Cross, No Crown*: A Study of the Atonement. Garden City, N.Y.: Doubleday and Co., Inc., 1957, 216 pp.

Wright, Martin, "Christian Pacifism," *Theology,* July, 1936.

Wright, R. F., "The Sword and the Cross," a brief historical exegesis from the early Fathers to the present time, *Churchman,* July, 1939.

Appendix

LIST OF OLD TESTAMENT REFERENCES

The following key is used to differentiate passages, though precision in this matter is impossible:

*   Gathered or die in peace.
** Perfect heart or equivalent.
†   Non war-like, or peace as opposed to war, yet sometimes more.
†† Vow a vow.
‡   Ask or inquire about welfare.
‡‡ Peace-offering.
§   "Well" — in good health.
§§ "Hold peace" in sense of not talking; root is not shalom.
x   Passages of more than usual interest.

Genesis
    8:8-11
* 15:15 x
§§ 24:21
† 26:29, 31 x
† 28:21
§ 29:6
    33:18
§§ 34:5
† 34:21
† 37:4
§ 37:14
    41:16 x
† 42:11, 19, 31, 33, 34
    43:23
§ 43:27, 28
    44:17

Exodus
    4:18
§§ 14:14
    18:23
‡‡ 20:24
    22:2-14 x
‡‡ 24:5
‡‡ 29:28
‡‡ 32:6

Leviticus
‡‡ 3:1, 3, 6, 9
‡‡ 4:10, 26, 31, 35
‡‡ 6:12
‡‡ 7:11, 13, 14, 15, 18, 20, 21, 29, 32, 33, 34, 37
‡‡ 9:4, 18, 22

§§ 10:3
‡‡ 10:14
‡‡ 17:5
‡‡ 19:5
‡‡ 22:21
‡‡ 23:19
    24:11
† 26:6 x

Numbers
    1:6
    2:12
    6:26 x
‡‡ 6:14
‡‡ 7
‡‡ 10:10
‡‡ 15:8
    25:12 x

Job
    5:23, 24
    8:6
    9:4
§§ 11:3
§§ 13:5, 13
    15:21 x
    21:9 x
    22:21
    25:2 x
§§ 33:31, 33

Psalms
    4:8
    7:4
    28:3
    29:11
    31:23
    34:14
    35:12, 20, 27
    37:11, 21, 37
    38:3
§§ 39:2, 12
    41:9, 12
†† 50:14
    55:18
    62:12
†† 65:1
    72:3, 7
    73:3
    76:2
    83:1
    85:8, 10 x
§§ 109:1
†† 116:14, 18
    119:165
    120:6, 7
    122:6, 7, 8
    125:5
    128:6
    147:14

Proverbs
    3:2, 17
‡‡ 7:14
§§ 11:12

    11:31
    12:21
    13:13, 21
†   16:7
§§ 17:28

Ecclesiastes
†   3:8 x
†† 5:4 x

Song of Solomon
    8:10 x

Isaiah
    1:23
†   2:1-4
    9:6, 7 x
    11:1-10
    26:3, 12 x
    27:5 x
    32:17, 18 x
    33:7
§§ 36:21
    38:17 x
    39:8 x
    41:3 x
§§ 42:14
    42:19
    44:26, 28
    45:7 x
    48:18-22 x
    52:7 x
    53:5 x
    54:10, 13 x
    55:12 x
    57:2, 18, 19, 21 x
    59:8 x
    60:17 x
    60:20
§§ 62:1, 6
§§ 64:12
    65:25
    66:6, 12 v

Jeremiah
    4:10
§§ 4:19

    6:14 x
    8:11, 15 x
    9:8 x
    12:5, 12 x
    14:13, 19 x
    15:5 x
    16:5 x
    16:18
    18:20
    20:10
    23:17 x
    25:37 x
    28:9 x
    29:7, 11 x
    30:5 x
    32:18
    33:6, 9 x
    34:5
    38:4, 22 x
    50:29
    51:6

Lamentations
    3:17

Ezekiel
    7:25
    13:10, 16 x
    34:25 x
    37:26 x

Daniel
    4:1
    5:26
    6:25, 26
    10:19
    11:21, 24

Hosea
    2:18
    9:7

Joel
None

Amos
    1:6, 9

‡‡ 5:22
    9:11ff.

Obadiah
  7

Jonah
None

Micah
  3:5

†   4:1-4
    5:5 x

Nahum
    1:12, 15

Habakkuk
None

Zephaniah
§§ 1:7
    3:9 x

Haggai
  2:6-9 x

Zechariah
†   3:10
    6:13
    8:10, 12, 16, 19 x
    9:10

Malachi
  2:5, 6 x

LIST OF NEW TESTAMENT REFERENCES

Only two differentiations are used: §§ for "Hold peace" and x as before.

Matthew
  5:9
  10:13, 34
§§ 20:31
§§ 26:63

Mark
§§ 1:25
§§ 3:4
§§ 4:39
  5:34
§§ 9:34
  9:50
§§ 10:48
§§ 14:61

Luke
  1:79
  2:14, 29
§§ 4:35
  7:50
  8:48
  10:5, 6
  11:21
  12:51
§§ 14:4
  14:32

§§ 18:39
  19:38
§§ 19:40
  19:42
§§ 20:26

John
  14:27 x
  16:33 x
  20:19, 21, 26

Acts
  9:31
  10:36 x
§§ 11:18
§§ 12:17
  12:20
§§ 15:13
  15:33
  16:36
§§ 18:9
  24:2

Romans
  1:7
  2:10
  3:17

  5:1
  8:6, 22-25
  12:18
  14:17, 19
  15:13, 33
  16:20

I Corinthians
  1:3
  2:9
  7:15
§§ 14:30
  14:33
  16:11

II Corinthians
  1:2
  13:11

Galatians
  1:3
  5:22
  6:16

Ephesians
  1:2
  2:14, 15, 17 x

4:3
6:15, 23

Philippians
1:2
4:7 x
4:9

Colossians
1:2
1:20
3:15

I Thessalonians
1:1
5:3, 13, 23

II Thessalonians
1:2
3:16

I Timothy
1:2

II Timothy
1:2
2:22

Titus
1:4

Philemon
3

Hebrews
7:1-2 x
11:31
12:11, 14
13:20

James
2:16
3:17, 18 x

I Peter
1:2
3:11
5:14

II Peter
1:2
3:13-14 x

I John
None

II John
3

III John
15

Jude
2